GINGER
EAST ᴛᴏ WEST

GINGER
EAST TO WEST

A COOK'S TOUR
with Recipes, Techniques & Lore

by

Bruce Cost

with a foreword by
Barbara Tropp

illustrated by Amy Pertschuk

ARIS BOOKS

Berkeley, Los Angeles

DEDICATION
For Jennifer, Eliza and Lynn
In Memory of Virginia Lee

Cover Design by Jeanne Jambu
Book Design by Fifth Street Design Associates
The bindings on this book are sewn for extra strength

Library of Congress Cataloging in Publication Data

Cost, Bruce, 1945–
  Ginger East to West.

  Bibliography: p.
  Includes indexes.
  1. Ginger.   2. Cookery (Ginger)   I. Title.
TX407.G56C67   1984   641.6'383   84-2842
ISBN 0-943186-06-4

Aris Books/Harris Publishing Company, Inc.
1621 Fifth Street
Berkeley, CA 94710

First Printing April 1984
2 4 6 8 9 7 5 3
Manufactured in the United States of America

CONTENTS

RECIPE INDEX

Vegetables

Pickles, Relishes, and Condiments

Gingerbread

Desserts and Confections

Beverages

Acknowledgements

Thanks first to my close friend Henry Cha, who, in 1966 at the New Shun Lee Restaurant on the Upper West Side of Manhattan, pointed out that the lobster dish we were eating was seasoned with fresh ginger—a substance whose existence I had never before considered. My deepest gratitude to the late, wonderfully wise Virginia Lee, who taught me that ginger not only went with lobster, but with every imaginable food.

I express my thanks to those directly responsible for this book: Isaac Cronin, who immediately liked the idea and introduced me to Aris publisher, John Harris; John, who loves the food herein and who supported my instincts from beginning to end; Sherry Virbila, who helped me get this book off the ground; my editor, Jay Harlow, for his dedication to shaping this book into a comprehensive whole; Amy Pertschuk for her finely rendered illustrations; also Mimi Luebbermann, Jeanne Jambu, Robin Cowan, Lisa Sommer, and the whole staff at Aris Books.

I am indebted to Don Harper of the Department of Oriental Languages, University of California at Berkeley, for his fascinating prime source material on ginger's use in Ancient China; to gastro-journalist and near Eastern language expert, Charles Perry for his etymological traces; and to Xiao Wei Xu for culling medicinal material from herbal texts. I appreciate the patience of Jean Bullock for allowing me afternoons of browsing in her Gourmet Guides bookshop.

I have Barbara Tropp to thank, not only for her foreword, but for her helpful comments about my first draft at a time when she was busy opening her new San Francisco restaurant, China Moon; also Ruth Reichl for considerable support; Cathy Shen, Chellis Glendinning, and my favorite neighbor, Maria Vella; my wife, Lynn, who took time from her own editing work to help me unclog several passages. From my old homestead: Gilda Lyons, and Randy Chu of Mandarin Foods in Poughkeepsie.

Fresh ginger authorities who guided me include: Frieda Caplan, produce wholesaler extraordinaire, of Los Angeles; Ray Borton of the California Department of Food and Agriculture; Bob Sbragia; Joe Carcione, the "Greengrocer" of San Francisco; Banana King Louie; and Charley Bettencourt, exotics authority of the San Francisco produce terminals. Knowledgeable retailers include: Glen Ysuda of the Berkeley Bowl Supermarket; the people at the American Fish Market in Japantown; and Edmund Seto among the many helpful merchants in Chinatown.

I am grateful for the ginger information from: Phillip E. Heald of the Australian Trade Commission; Derryck Cox, Jamaican Trade Commissioner; Tom Burns of the American Spice Trade Association; Louise Erickson of Lewis and Neale; Robert Tuchman, Old Tyme Ginger Beer; Canada Dry; Schweppes; and thanks to Anne Kupper of Williams-Sonoma.

I especially thank Bay Area pastry and baking experts, Marion Cunningham, Lindsey Shere, Jim Dodge, Karen Shapiro, and Alan Oswald. Also, thanks to gingerbread enthusiast, Helen Gustafson. Their gingerbread recipes make that chapter a small treasure.

B.C.

Foreword

I don't know what it is that makes a native-born American yearn for things like ginger, cultivate fantasies of ancient China, and seek some road in life that will mesh the exotics of other lands with the realities of everyday living in a very Western city like San Francisco. Whether it be past lives or a modern and decidedly international appetite that begs for some foreign spice to give greater dimension to Mom's apple pie, a few of us seem fated to walk the earth with a Western face and an Eastern heart. Bruce Cost and I—people who are remarkably unsimilar in many other ways—share this peculiarity. We are lured by the tastes and secrets of other cultures as if by a magnet, and feel compelled to then share the treasures with our own kind. We both use the kitchen and the act of feeding friends as the crucible for this sort of cultural transformation. Swirling soy sauce, rice vinegar, and bits of minced ginger in a dipping sauce for a fresh-steamed Pacific crab, the message seems to be, "Taste this! Eat a bit of what you know and what you don't. Open your eyes through the tastes on your tongue!"

The tastes on my own tongue are now, more often than not, hinting of ginger. I am passionate about it, this sensation of hot-clean-cool that comes full-force and without coaxing from the golden-fleshed rhizome of the ginger plant. The taste is like the flower put out by the plant when the rhizome is left underground to sprout—a burst of sensuous, bright color whose beauty is in directness, not subtlety.

My personal "ginger odyssey" began, I suspect, on the New Jersey Turnpike. Returning home weekly to the monochromatic suburbs from my grandmother's apartment in the then intriguingly ethnic city of Newark, there was on the left-hand side of the road the great Canada Dry plant with its overgrown ginger ale bottle looming on the roof, lit brightly for us kids to see. How many baby bellyaches were washed away by this bubbly stuff? I suspect quite a few, not a small number of which were inspired by lustful, pubescent gorgings on gingerbread—the dark, sultry mass that came oftentimes in a tin and responded favorably and squishily to prying fingers. Somewhat later, my appetites civilized to a reasonable degree, I turned to making gingerbread cookies with boyfriends and hanging them on Christmas trees. My first and best ones were gingerbread ladies baked with stars on their heads, that fell with a soft "plop" in the middle of the night on account of a too-tender dough.

Then came the years in Taiwan as a graduate student, and my tastes for ginger turned Asian. Learning to eat was my mission and ginger was everywhere. Slivered in a web of yellow-gold threads as the topping for a clear-steamed fish . . . exciting a "lion's head" meatball into tasty wakefulness as one plucked it with chopsticks from its stewed cabbage mane . . . chopped fine into a forcemeat for Chinese New Year's dumplings that lent an extra freshness to the holidays. We grew ginger in the front courtyard and nibbled on the baby shoots to avert a stomach ache. We arranged ginger flowers in a celadon bowl for the sitting room. It was the zesty yang counterpoint to the cold and quiet yin moods in our lives and our meals.

Life goes on and the odyssey of the tastebuds with it. I have recently returned to Asia, hunting for signs and tastes of ginger with the foreword for Bruce's book in mind. In Taiwan, I saw market after outdoor market overflowing with summer ginger—long "hands" with rosy fingertips and pale gold skin, striking in any case but especially so surrounded by amethyst Chinese eggplant, jade long-beans, and the ruby-colored flesh of fresh pork that makes a Taipei market the most jewel-like in all of Chinese-speaking Asia. And then in Hong Kong it was the season for Shanghai crabs. Wooden bucket-fuls of the hairy little beasts with their thick shells and prized flesh were sold on every corner and mounted as a colossal centerpiece in the dining room of the Sichuan restaurant where we ate dinner one night, dipping the snippets of meat into a tiny bowl of hot vinegar riddled with mashed ginger, our tongues and lips singing, our fingers fatigued from the battle with the shells.

On into mainland China, ginger was a rare familiar note in an otherwise very foreign land. Landing in Kunming at dusk and driving into town amidst the uncanny swishing sounds of bicyclers returning home from work en masse, the bright orange-red ginger flowers planted dead-center down the middle of the road shone out like a beacon in the waning light. And the next day ever more so, against the grey-green-blue that is the color wheel of communist China. A similar juxtaposition awaited us next in Kuilin. Arriving again by air, this time smack in the middle of a fantasy land of whimsically tipped mountains that sprout magically from the flat plain as if by the design of some playful giant, my eye was drawn to the flaming, flowering ginger bordering the small airstrip. Sitting on the ground with my back propped against the comfort of the plants, I stared for the better part of an hour at the astonishing scene, feeling a kinship with the painters whose scrolls I had so meticulously pored over as a student and whose fascination with the landscape was suddenly my own.

On this particular trip there was more ginger to see than to eat, as my route snaked eastward across China's southern half. In Kuilin's depressingly poor free market, a few sticks of lanky ginger were aggressively peddled by a broad-faced, dark-skinned boy from the countryside, while the silent granny next to him, smiling and toothless, gestured encouragingly to the knobs of dried ginger meticulously spread out on an ancient, dusty plastic bag. The young man's ginger was bought by a pretty girl clutching a fistful of perky scallions and a just-killed carp, the old lady's by a crone probably older than she. In Suzhou, the market was a bit cleaner and cheerier and the ginger-seller middle-aged. I bought from him a bit of ginger and some pungent strips of garlic chives, both "foreign spices," insisted our Suzhou-born guide, whose nose soared equal to my spirits at the thought of chopping them into our dreary hotel dinner.

Now home in California, my Asian and ginger-attuned heart comfortable in this very Western setting, I page through the manuscript of Bruce's book with a deep sense of pleasure. Yesterday, Bruce and I were walking through San Francisco Chinatown, two ginger-wise Westerners shopping for our dinners in a sea of foreign faces. Today, our hungers express themselves beyond the bounds of our Chinatown jaunts and our own kitchens. I, with one book behind me, am now consumed with opening a restaurant to bring my tastes—ginger among them—to a wider audience than the good friends who cluster around my single wok. Bruce, having finished the act of writing a meaningful, wonderfully focused book, is on the brink of seeing his knowledge and talents transmitted to a large group of cooks and cookbook-lovers who will pick up this volume with justifiable enthusiasm, hunger, and the sense of a fine adventure about to begin.

From the hot, buttery spiciness of Bruce's "Real Ginger Beef" to the sweet madcap of Jim Dodge's "Victorian Gingerbread House," this is an appetite-arousing volume. Bruce has taken the time to sniff the ginger with his excellent nose and savor it. The result is a book full of spicy promise—a treasure for the lively cook as well as the reader of lively cookbooks. I welcome him to the club of good-cooking missionaries and award him the title "Master of Ginger."

Barbara Tropp
San Francisco
Year of the Rat, 1984

Introduction

Years ago it would have been easier to write a book about ginger than to find a piece of it fresh. I had always been willing to expend the energy because the cooking I did was Chinese, and fresh ginger is mandatory. Almost suddenly I noticed it was becoming easier to find—in fact, little knobs of it began to appear in supermarket chain stores. Since everyone in America would soon be wheeling their shopping carts past this strange little "root," I decided that a small book showing how ginger is used around the world would appeal to American cooks.

Up until now, ginger to most Americans was the powder they pulled out of their spice cabinets at Christmas and blended with molasses to make cakes and cookies. Occasionally, when I mentioned writing an entire book about ginger, people—either out of bewilderment or concern for my plight—would dredge up all the old ginger stories they could think of. This was somehow reassuring, and had its nice moments. Everyone's childhood included the gingerbread house that tempted Hansel and Gretel; or the gingerbread man—the sassy underdog we cheered—who ran like the wind into the jaws of a fox. Gingerbread men were the first baked goods many of us ever produced. During an early discussion of this book, a friend's face suddenly lit up at the memory of spending hours at age 14 making a gingerbread map the size of a card table "with all the capitals in the right place." Yet fresh ginger, a staple to some three billion people, was simply not part of our experience.

Ginger is rapidly losing its holiday-time identity. In 1971, when I moved from Manhattan to the village of Rhinebeck, New York, I suggested to the only grocer in town that he order some "ginger root." He looked at me as though I spoke a different tongue and went on filing his bills. When I left in 1981, not only was ginger stocked, the checkout people knew its price without having to yell to the back of the store. Fresh ginger is widely available today mainly because of the growth in the population of Asian and Latin American people, for whom it is a staple. But the current explosion of interest in international food throughout the country has added to the demand. Growers in the United States now produce a fresh ginger crop of matchless quality in Hawaii. It is jetted over the Pacific to the mainland like pineapples, by the ton, to meet domestic demand.

We've certainly waited awhile to learn to use and love ginger. Our fellow cooks in Asia have used fresh ginger for perhaps 7,000 years. Where its use originated, whether in China or India (if either), is still debated. It is an unparalleled endorsement that, of all the aromatic foodstuffs that must have been tried during the thousands of years it took these two giant neighbors to develop their distinctly different cuisines, ginger has stood the test of time in both. In fact, their dependence on it is the most fundamental link in their cooking.

Shortly after I began this book, smug in my knowledge of fresh ginger, I quickly came to realize I had tackled a big subject. Fresh ginger is more widely used than I had imagined. I found that the dried spice, which I had disparaged as a mere substitute, has a story of its own that cuts a swath through Western history; and that sometimes where dried ground ginger is used, as it is in the Middle East, it is used to advantage. I knew vaguely that ginger was healthy—nothing with such a fresh fragrance could possibly hurt you. But I had no idea that ginger, as much as any substance could be, was a panacea in both the East and the West from the birth of medicine until relatively recently, and that it is still an important medicinal in much of the world.

A recent tongue-in-cheek article on fad foods in *The New York Times* declared this "the year of ginger." I could see the humor—even after having spent more than a year writing a book about it. We are up to our gullets in food trends. But after tracing the history of this plant around the world and through thousands of years, witnessing its adoption by culture after culture, I must conclude that if using ginger is a fad, so is walking upright.

Bruce Cost
San Francisco
February, 1984

Author's Notes
On Assembling Recipes for a Ginger Cookbook

Choosing recipes was the pure fun of preparing this book, for me as well as for an assortment of tasters. Ginger is part of so many noteworthy dishes that what to leave out becomes problematic. Even now, in the book's final stages, people call me with ginger recipes—a few minutes ago, a pear and ginger soup was mine for the asking.

Narrow criteria had to be established at the outset. The most basic is that the recipes represent the use of ginger in cultures that have depended on it; a culture's use of ginger can be a means of understanding its entire way of cooking. The recipes also had to combine ginger with other staples in ways that represent each cuisine's most characteristic flavors. I favored recipes that offer potentially new tastes to adventurous cooks willing to try exotic combinations. Above all, the food from these recipes had to prove delicious to me and to all the others who ate a lot of ginger for the sake of this project.

More than being a handy guide to an important food, this book is for people to cook from. Part of my enjoyment of food is the insight I gain into a culture by eating what its people eat. My favorite cookbooks respect authenticity. Books that dramatically adjust ingredients and proportions to what are perceived to be Western tastes betray their readers. I look back on my first few years of cooking Chinese food as a time when I had to read between the lines of available cookbooks to discover that this indeed was a fascinating cuisine. Beef with broccoli, seasoned with a dime-sized slice of ginger and a smidgen of minced garlic, turned out not to be China's number one dish.

Authenticity of ingredients causes big problems to anyone writing an international cookbook, particularly if most of the recipes are not Western. Some important ingredients are not yet available in this country; some ingredients that are available, like frogs and eels, are not the staples they are elsewhere and make some of us squeamish. Ingredients that we commonly use, such as garlic, chilis, oils, and fats, are not necessarily consumed here in the proportions they are in other cultures.

The problem of food categories is no less vexing. Since Americans eat a lot of beef, should a cookbook on cuisines that traditionally use little beef nevertheless have a substantial section devoted to it? Should sweets be gathered from the Asian cultures, for whom dessert at the end of a meal is not a concept, simply to provide a dessert section to conform to Western tastes?

I decided not to include recipes that require unavailable ingredients. Though I was tempted, to do so would have served no practical purpose. A few cookbooks I prize, like Alan Davidson's meticulously informative *Fish and Fish Dishes of Laos*, are virtually unusable unless you toss them in a suitcase and head for some far corner of the earth. I almost had to sacrifice recipes calling for fresh galangal, ginger's cousin, but fortunately it is now available in Asian markets. Some recipes do call for ingredients that are not in everyone's supermarket, and might require some hunting or a trip to an unfamiliar part of town. For these I have provided a Special Ingredients section.

A few of the recipes include foods that we euphemistically call foreign delicacies, even when they may be the major source of protein for twelve million people. If most of our fellow humans relish a particular food, and it is important to a ginger-based cuisine, I included it. I prefer to give someone the opportunity to skip over a recipe for eel or pork kidney than to have that person miss a chance to try a food that has delighted many for a long time.

I took pains to provide recipes with the proportions of ingredients unaltered from the way they are enjoyed in their country of origin. In a couple of cases this meant restoring the integrity of representative ginger recipes that have obviously been Westernized, or have lost something in the translation (like most of their garlic or chili peppers). A few of the recipes are complete hybrids that sprang from the test kitchen.

The recipes are divided by regions of the world, just as I have divided the narrative, so that the recipes illustrate the text. If you intend to use this book strictly as a cookbook, the recipes from each region work best together as a meal. (An index on page vii divides the recipes into more traditional categories.)

Gingerbread has its own chapter because of its unusually lore-filled history. The subject is entertaining and a rich symbol for the incorporation of Eastern spices into the cuisines of the West. Candied ginger, ginger drinks, and ginger as medicine each have a chapter with recipes.

I would take the credit for balancing the recipes nicely among all food categories, except that the use of ginger divides itself conveniently among everything from soups to pickles to desserts. The number of seafood dishes is perhaps disproportionately large, and there are fewer beef recipes than pork, both of which reflect the cultures studied as well as my personal preferences.

I.
ABOUT GINGER

The Official Ginger

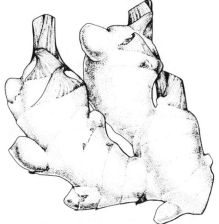

Hawaiian "Baby" Ginger

As anyone who writes about ginger hastens to point out, ginger is not a root, it is a rhizome—a tuber-like stem with roots of its own. To call ginger "ginger root," or as it is sometimes written, "gingerroot," is simply incorrect.

There is only one ginger species, *Zingiber officinale*, the official ginger, which we use fresh or dried and ground as a spice. It is presumed to be native to tropical Asia, but no one agrees precisely where. Ginger has grown only as a cultivated plant for thousands of years, and its cultivation has spread to suitable climates throughout the world. It grows best partially shaded, on a slope no higher than 4,800 feet, in rich sandy loams with good drainage—preferably volcanic. High temperatures, high humidity, and heavy rainfall are musts during the growing season. (To grow ginger at home, see the Appendix.)

The plant looks tropical and has a passing resemblance to bamboo. It grows up to three feet tall with thin, pointed, nine-inch leaves and small yellow to yellow-green flowers with touches of purple. The rhizome creeps as it grows along by sprouting new stalks. It is not a crop grown from its seed, and about 25 percent of the harvested rhizomes are saved as seed pieces. Rhizomes grown to be dried for grinding into spice are harvested at the end of nine months when the foliage turns brown. Those to be used fresh, which are by far th' majority, can be dug up as soon as three weeks after planting.

The Ginger Family

Z. *officinale* is a member of the Zingiberaceae family of plants, many of which have distinguished themselves as food and medicines since antiquity. These include the rhizomes turmeric and galangal, and the seed pods of several species of the ginger family, known as cardamoms. The following is a guide to these gingers, including a few others that have been linked to ginger down through the ages.

Turmeric

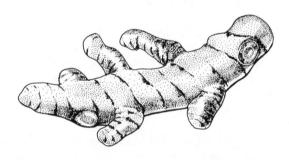

Turmeric (*Curcuma longa*), often called "Indian saffron" in the Middle East and "yellow ginger" in the Far East, is native to tropical Asia where it is used fresh as well as dried. Turmeric has been a highly valued medicinal and spiritual tonic in India and China for thousands of years. The flavor of both fresh and dried turmeric is reminiscent of fragrant wood. In the United States it is familiar as the yellow coloring in mustard and commercial curry powders, and is sold mostly in powdered form. If one has access to an Indian or Southeast Asian market, dried rhizomes can be bought and ground to taste, yielding much more flavor. Turmeric can also be purchased fresh in Southeast Asian markets.

Two lesser-known Zingiberaceae of the tumeric type are zedoary (*Curcuma zedoaria*), an Asian medicinal valued in medieval Europe as a remedy for the plague, and mango ginger (*Curcuma amada*), which has a mango scent.

Galangal

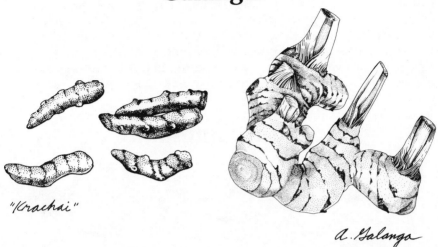

"Krachai"

a. Galanga

Galangal (*Alpinia* and *Kaempferia* spp.), "galingale" to the English, includes a group of rhizomes widely used for food and medicine in Asia. Galangal made it to Europe in the Middle Ages, where it was used with abandon as a seasoning, before being dropped from use. Its medicinal properties, including its ability to "help those weak in the sports of Venus,"[1] sold it in the West.

Alpinia galanga, also known as "Thai ginger," "Java Root," or "laos,"* is the largest and best known of the galangals. The Chinese cultivate it for medicine, but it is used fresh as a major seasoning, sometimes to the exclusion of ginger, in Thailand and Java. The standard cure for stomach upset in Thailand is to take *A. galanga* grated with lime juice.

A. galanga is also used, although to a lesser extent, in Indian, Middle Eastern, and North African cuisine. Paula Wolfert encountered it in Morocco and thought it "tastes like a cross between ginger and cardomom." If you want to test this, *A. galanga* can be purchased dried, in slices or powdered, in Thai or Vietnamese food stores. Packages are marked "galanga" or "laos" and sometimes *Kha*. As of this writing, fresh galangal has very recently become available, at least in California.

Other galangals of the genus *Kaempferia*, known for good reason as "camphor roots," or *kentjur* to the Indonesians, and *krachai* to the Thais, are important in Asian food and medicine. The small finger-like rhizomes are cooked whole in curries throughout South Asia. Curiously,

---

* The Indonesian terms laos or laos powder have nothing to do with the country Laos, where the rhizome is called "lang uas." Besides laos, the Indonesians call it *lenguas*.

this lesser galangal is not mentioned in books on Indian cuisine in this country, and only hinted at in Southeast Asian food books. As one book states in an introductory section on ingredients, "it can be left out of recipes without great harm," advice that was followed for the rest of the book.[2] Despite this lack of guidance, these skinny, ringed rhizomes are available fresh in the United States for those who want to cook with them. In Asian and Indian markets they are often referred to as "Indian ginger."[3]

Cardamoms

E. Cardamomum

Cardamoms (*Amomum* and *Elettaria* spp.) are the seed pods of the Zingiberaceae. At least a dozen varieties of cardamoms are important to the food and medicine of Asia, India, and the Middle East. The most familiar is the luxurious *Elettaria cardamomum*, best purchased as dried green pods which contain about a dozen seeds—used as breath fresheners in India. The seeds are sold separately, whole or ground. To preserve fragrance, it is best to grind the seeds as the need arises. This spice is second only to saffron in price.

Less prized, though important, are the bitter black cardomom (*Elettaria cardamomum*, var. *major*),[4] the smell of which has been likened to old shoes; and the notorious "grains of paradise" (*Amomum melegueta*), indigenous to West Africa. As their name suggests, these grains are a valued aphrodisiac. Their popularity rose and fell with galangal in Medieval Europe, where they were believed to prevent drunkenness and, if unsuccessful, to cure hangovers.

Mioga Ginger

Mioga ginger (*Zingiber mioga*) grows in more temperate climates than its cousins. It is native to China and maybe to Japan, though most likely it was brought there from China. The ancient Chinese cultivated it, then let it go wild. Today it is still valued in Japan, where the spring shoots are pickled and dyed red. *Hajikami-shōga* or "blushing ginger," as it is called, is costly and used a sprig at a time for garnish. In

Japanese markets in the United States, a six-ounce jar is a shade under ten dollars, and only the base of the shoot is edible since the top two-thirds is fibrous.

Near Fresno, California, Japanese farmers grow mioga ginger for select markets in Japanese communities. The shoots, which appear briefly in the spring, are harvested and eaten fresh as part of a Buddhist tradition.

Ornamentals

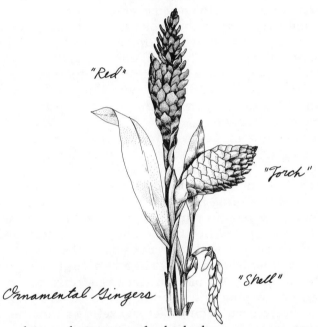

"Red"

"Torch"

"Shell"

Ornamental Gingers

Other cultivated gingers, of which there are many, can be found at any large flower market where spectacular varieties of these blooming exotics may be purchased. Most arrive here from Hawaii, though ginger plants are popular ornamentals throughout Asia.

Other unrelated plants have sometimes been associated with ginger. Ginseng, which bears some resemblance to ginger, is a root that grows in colder climates, and is not related, though in medical lore it is linked to ginger. A plant known as wild ginger grows in the United States and is likened to ginger in books on living off the land. It is not a member of the family, but a birthwort of the family Aristolochiaceae. Two African trees, the gingerbread palm, or "doom palm," which bears a gingerbread-flavored fruit, and the gingerbread tree, which grows a large "gingerbread plum," are also unrelated to ginger.

GINGER'S ENGLISH ROOTS

Ginger spiced up the language as well as the cuisine when it invaded England sometime before the Norman Conquest of 1066. The use of this seasoning became so pervasive in the Middle Ages that the word ginger became synonymous with spice in certain contexts.[5] It even had a cannister of its own at the table, a concept that startles those of us who thought salt and pepper were a mandate from when human beings first sat down to eat. Besides adding flavor to food, ginger's ability to warm people up and stimulate their circulation was common knowledge. "It heateth in the third degree," according to Elizabethan herbalist John Gerard. Ginger, in other words, meant zing to food, life, and conversation.

Today the noun ginger means pep or liveliness for the British, and there are vestiges of this usage in New England. The verb form, which means "to pep up," or "give life to," is also bandied about. Webster's example, "to ginger up the tourist trade," is an appropriate one considering England's experience administering tropical islands. Applying the name Ginger to redheaded females because of their supposed hot temperaments was standard in Elizabethan England, like Red for redheaded males. In fact, red hair today is described as gingerous. The adjective gingery, when used to describe one's complexion, means strong brown or ruddy; a gingery morning is invigorating. The adverb gingerly, meaning cautiously, seems contradictory; yet, as a modifier applied strictly to dance, it meant lively but graceful.

Eventually, to "ginger it up" or "add spice to your life" meant more than just stimulating your palate. Gerard wrote that ginger "provoketh Venerie."[6] Ginger thus gave us "racy" as in "racily clad." The English called knobs of ginger "races," from the Portuguese-Spanish *raices*, meaning root.[7] Food laced with ginger came to be called racy as well as spicy, both of which suggest all of ginger's qualities. In the United States the predominant connotation of racy is "suggestive," while in Britain it can as easily mean lively, strong flavored, or piquant—another word that may have broader meaning due to an early link with ginger.[8]

The Fresh Ginger Market: What's Available

Buying fresh ginger no longer represents the problem it did a few years ago. While people may not idle away their hours debating where to get the best "Hawaiian," "Fijian," or "Costa Rican," these are among the varieties now available.

All of the fresh ginger sold in the United States comes from the same sources. Most enters through California, the biggest market, from the tropical Pacific, and arrives seasonally depending on which side of the equator it comes from. In Asian and other specialty markets Hawaiian ginger is clearly dominant in winter and spring, although it is available in some stages throughout the year. Fijian is the best in late summer and fall. Other gingers fill in the gaps. That there is a difference is apparent to West Coast "exotics" wholesalers who, in cooperation with Hawaiian and Fijian growers, have set up a grading system for the finest rhizomes. In fact, Hawaii has set up a ginger growers trade association, and is actively pursuing the rapidly growing United States market. We get our ginger from the sources listed below:

Hawaii (mature top grade: winter to late spring). This is the top of the line. According to wholesalers, the lowest grade Hawaiian is as good as or better than any other. Not only is the rhizome of high quality, it's also flown here fresh. At its peak, in January and February, the huge shiny tubers are a visual treat in Asian markets. If not broken, one individual mass of rhizomes may weigh over five pounds. At this age the pale golden sweet flesh is low in fiber and medium hot. It is also costly when it makes its splashy entrance, but the price drops steadily as April and the end of the season approaches.

"Young" or "baby" ginger (early summer for the true "baby ginger" to early fall). The Hawaiian season begins, in a sense, in early summer with the arrival of the beautiful, translucent-skinned "young" or

"Number 1" Hawaiian

"baby" ginger. The rhizomes are cream colored with pink-tipped shoots, and at this time appear only in Asian markets. They are expensive and have a wonderful texture, but their flavor is undeveloped and lacks bite. They are best pickled, preserved in syrup, candied, or cooked like a vegetable as the Chinese do in a few dishes.

Fiji (late summer to early winter). Fijian ginger, though it has neither the spectacular visual appearance nor the size of midwinter Hawaiian, is excellent. Its skin is somewhat rough in texture and light colored with occasional traces of red soil. Most importantly, the pale flesh is full flavored, hot, with a pleasing seamless texture maintained throughout its growing season.

Other sources include **Taiwan** and **the Phillipines**. The United States is not their major market, so ginger is purchased and shipped on a spot basis, and the quality varies. The ginger shipped by boat may arrive a little tired; but if fresh, both varieties are excellent. **Nicaragua**, **Costa Rica**, and **Guatemala** grow winter crops, the best of which appear in Latin markets, and the worst of which are shipped with other winter produce throughout the United States. Wholesalers mention a "Bluefields" brand from Central America, which is a selection of the region's finest, and is exported by one packer. It is even purchased from time to time by Asian retailers, and is evidently cultivated by Chinese farmers, which is the case with a lot of Latin American ginger. **Brazil**, where ginger is heavily consumed, and **Ecuador** supply some American markets in the summer. A little ginger arrives from the southernmost reaches of **Mexico**, but

Figi Ginger

it is not a staple of Mexican cooking. When I discovered mountains of fresh ginger in Mexican markets in the Mission District of San Francisco, a dealer explained they carry it for Central and South American customers.

China and **India** raise the bulk of the world's ginger crop, but we rarely see it fresh—except for the occasional shriveled rhizomes shipped from China. Most of their green (fresh) ginger is consumed by their citizens, though they are the world's leaders in processing and exporting the dried spice.

United States Mainland. Domestic ginger? Not yet. While one authoritative garden guide lists twelve climate zones, all in California, where *Zingiber officinale* can be grown, none is being raised commercially. Chinese farmers have been a major agricultural force in California since the Gold Rush; one suspects that it would have been grown by now if it could be, particularly since those who first arrived were from regions in Southern China where ginger has been raised for thousands of years.

Dried Ginger: The Spice

Dried ground ginger should never be substituted in recipes calling for fresh ginger. But fresh does not always mean best. In India, both forms are used, sometimes together, and have separate names. In the Middle East, dried ginger has been used to the exclusion of fresh through centuries of culinary refinement.

As with any spice, dried ginger is best freshly ground. Curiously, many food authorities who insist on grinding their own pepper and grating their own nutmeg ignore this requirement for ginger. Yet its fragrance deteriorates at least as rapidly as other spices. Spice dealers in urban areas and Indian food stores sell what are called "hands" of dried ginger, and Chinese apothecaries carry it in slices. Some shops may grind it for you, or you can do it yourself with a spice grinder.

The Producers

India has been the top producer of dried ginger since the dawn of the spice trade, though Indians use mostly the fresh rhizome in their own cooking. Their main market has always been the Middle East, which consumes the lion's share of this spice. Europe's frenzied use of ginger throughout the Middle Ages kept Indian growers busy until the sixteenth century, when Spain and Portugal decided to grow their own ginger in Jamaica and West Africa. Only recently, India has become the main supplier to the United States.

Jamaica and its ginger plantations were taken from Spain by England in the 1670s. Slaves planted and harvested thousands of tons of ginger. They had to hand peel each rhizome and set it in the sun to dry. The result was a product of high purity and fine fragrance. Jamaican ginger was marketed as the world's finest and filled the demands of Europe and North America. However, according to the American Spice Trade Association, little Jamaican ginger has come into this country since the early 1960s because of the high cost of labor; Jamaican peeling methods have practically priced it out of the market.

It is still available and is indeed a superior dried ginger, and Jamaica has plans to revitalize its industry.

China's entrance into Western markets was a major blow to the Jamaican ginger industry. Though the Chinese use dried ginger only for medicine, China has taken over the market for the top grades by offering a seasoning of comparable purity to Jamaica's, at less than half the price. The Chinese rhizomes are not shipped whole, but come dried, in thick slices.

Sierra Leone and Nigeria have competed in the dried ginger market since the height of the European spice trade. The pungency of their product has rendered it best for extraction. Australia is the market's newest entrant, offering a complete line of ginger products. As yet, only its candies and preserves have come West.

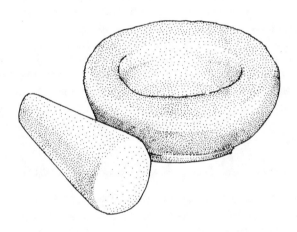

Processed Ginger

Sierra Leone

The United States is dependent on the West African nation of Sierra Leone for ginger to be used for extraction. It is not computer chips, but it is a bigger industry than one might guess. West African dried ginger has a high oil content, and these oils or oleoresins are separated as a sort of flavor concentrate. The carbonated beverage industries create a big demand for such concentrates, not just for ginger ale but for an array of soft drinks, tonics, and mixers. Ginger extract is a standard flavoring for commercial pickles and relishes, and the scent of the oil makes it valuable to cosmetics manufacturers. Commercial-grade powdered ginger (that which meets federal guidelines for volatile oils, starches, etc.) from Sierra Leone and elsewhere is what the trade calls "a silent partner" in formulas for sausages, baked goods and other desserts, condiments, pickles, and spice blends.

Australia's "Ginger Coast"

Australia's booming cooperative ginger growing and processing industry was established in the 1940s and is a source of unabashed pride. A few plants brought from China in 1923 flourished on the sunshine coast of Queensland, which is now known as the "ginger coast." Up to 1,500 people a day tour the Buderim ginger factory where crystalized ginger, ginger in syrup, waffle topping, marmalade, and sandwich spreads are manufactured under the Merrybud label. This factory also produces a ground dried ginger spice, and a whole rhizome for extract, neither of which reaches the United States.

The Buderim Ginger Growers Co-operative Association, Ltd., is described in promotional literature as "similar in character to those California organizations devoted to different types of nuts." Regardless of how they have assembled themselves, they cannot grow and preserve enough of their mild, fiberless preserved ginger to satisfy the sweet tooths of Great Britain, West Germany, Holland, Switzerland, and Norway. This pleasantly textured confection is now available in the United States plain or chocolate covered.

Buying, Storing, and Preparing Fresh Ginger

Fresh ginger becomes more widely available by the day. I could be accused of having a skewed outlook, since I can see San Francisco's Chinatown from my window, but my importer sources say they are now shipping the best varieties all over the country. Now that one can shop selectively for ginger rather than be thankful for whatever moldy little rhizomes are available, the following guide should be helpful.

Freshness. Like a potato, the harder the better; rhizomes that sit around become wrinkled and feel light. Those freshly harvested are rock-hard and noticeably weighty. The sheen of the skin is not a reliable indicator. Polished rhizomes from Hawaii, with taut smooth skin, are most certainly fresh, but Fijian rhizomes, with a rougher complexion, may also be fresh. Even rhizomes shipped in what the importers refer to as dirty condition can be perfectly good. Occasionally, ginger is shipped or stored in tightly sealed containers to preserve freshness, and mold grows where the knobs have broken off. If it's an emergency, and the moldy rhizome feels firm, you can buy it and scrape off the mold. But point it out to your greengrocer. Ginger keeps well, so this shouldn't happen.

Presently, ginger is best purchased at Asian markets. Chances are the quality will be higher, it will be fresher, and the price will be lower. Many non-Asian produce managers who are carrying ginger for the first time are not as apt to seek out Hawaiian ginger when it peaks in February if it's easier to get ginger as part of a winter produce shipment from Guatemala.

Maturity. As a rule, the longer the rhizome grows before harvesting, the more fibrous it becomes. More mature rhizomes will be more piquant, and to some extent, more fragrant and flavorful. Fibrous ginger hinders the fine cuts required by Chinese cooking; but where the ginger is to be grated, say for a Japanese or Korean dipping sauce, its extra flavor and heat may be preferable.

It is difficult to gauge maturity without slicing into the rhizome, but you can get a clue from the fibers that stick out from a freshly broken knob (young ginger won't have any fibers). Generally, older ginger is less rotund and more elongated, although this varies with the origin of the plant.

Size. Size is mostly a function of where the ginger is grown. Hawaiian ginger at any stage of maturity dwarfs other rhizomes. From a peeling and cutting standpoint, of course, the larger the better.

Color. Color, inside or out, also depends on where the ginger is grown, and neither indicates quality or maturity. The flesh ranges from pale golden to cream colored, and the skin from light beige to tan.

Flavor. Though not as pleasant as tasting Cabernet Sauvignon, I recommend comparing the flavors of gingers from different parts of the world; each is surprisingly distinct. All have a refreshing floral/medicinal dimension, and each has its own particular hotness. Some are sweet and some are dry. Rhizomes that sit around eventually lose their full-bodied fragrance, and will have a hot, flat, and slightly bitter flavor.

Storing Fresh Ginger

I have a library of Asian and Indian cookbooks containing myriad tips for storing fresh ginger, most of which are useless. It's not terribly perishable; it's no longer difficult to find; it's usually fresh when it hits the market; and anyone using this book should go through a couple of pounds a week at least! If it's fresh and firm to begin with and you plan to use it within a week, toss it into your vegetable crisper. To keep it longer, put it in a plastic bag with a paper towel to absorb the moisture that can cause mold, or put it in a paper bag inside a plastic bag for the same effect. It will be fine for two to three weeks, depending on how fresh it was when purchased.

In Chinese cooking, where texture is important, freezing fresh ginger is a mistake—it turns to mush. For ginger that is to be grated and juiced, or smashed, or blended, freezing is acceptable if you cannot buy it regularly. Pickling ginger in sherry or vodka is harmless, though it shouldn't be necessary.

Preparing Fresh Ginger

To cook with fresh ginger, you will need to prepare it as follows:

Peel. Ginger rhizomes can be peeled with a swivel-blade vegetable peeler or a paring knife. While some books state that the ginger skin has a neutral flavor, and recommend not peeling ginger, it is a simple refinement that is aesthetically important. However, there are two exceptions: the barely formed pale skin of young ginger need only be washed, and ginger slices that are added to sauces or to the cavities of poultry to be discarded need not be peeled. The peelings may be saved for juice in certain Chinese dishes (see below).

Slice. Ginger should be sliced across the fibers. Slices that are to be shredded, minced, or added to a dish as an ingredient should be as thin as possible.

Slicing fresh ginger

Shred. Also referred to as a match-stick cut, this must only be done with a sharp knife, preferably a French chef's knife or a Chinese cleaver, never a food processor or grater. Stack slices of thinly sliced ginger and cut into fine slivers. For shredding in quantity, the slices may be spread overlapping on the cutting board, like a deck of cards.

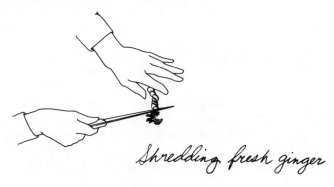

Shredding fresh ginger

Mince. Ginger that is finely diced should be prepared with a sharp knife. A food processor would ruin the crisp texture. It is easiest to first slice and shred the ginger, then line up the shreds and cut across into a fine dice. If the ginger is to be finely minced, chop further with the knife. Again, a heavy French chef's knife or Chinese cleaver works best. For less refined mincing or rough chopping simply smash a peeled ginger knob with the side of your knife and chop.

mincing fresh ginger

Grate. The Japanese manufacture graters specifically for ginger and wasabi (the familiar green horseradish root). These *oroshigane* are available in stainless steel, aluminum, or plastic at stores carrying Japanese cookware. The original graters were of a pottery material, and are quite attractive. The finest holes on an all-purpose Western grater are a poor substitute for these; it is better to use the chopping blade of a food processor, as the result is more akin to grated ginger than chopped or minced.

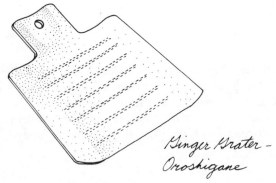

Ginger Grater - Oroshigane

Smash. Simply peel a small knob or cut a slice one-quarter-inch thick and smash it as you would a garlic clove.

Juice. Grate the ginger onto a cheesecloth, wrap the cloth around the ginger and squeeze. Or just take the ginger gratings and squeeze them in your hand into a measuring spoon. The Chinese make a ginger juice for use in their quenelle-like balls of puréed chicken or seafood by pouring boiling water over ginger peelings. Often a bruised scallion is added. This juice will retain its flavor for a week in a jar stored in the refrigerator.

Pound. A mortar and pestle are used to pound fresh ginger with other aromatics, toasted spices, and a little liquid or oil into a paste that is basic to both Southeast Asian and Indian cuisines. One of the main concerns of a Thai mother is said to be that the woman her son marries be adept at pounding as an indication that she's a good cook. I don't know the value an American mother places on her daughter-in-law's ability with a blender, but it works well for this purpose. A food processor works if the spices, if any, are ground before they are added.

Dry. You may dry your own ginger by peeling it and leaving it in the sun for ten days to two weeks. The Chinese save time by cutting the ginger into thick slices after peeling. Look for mature rhizomes— young ones don't have enough flavor. Dried rhizomes can be ground as needed in a spice grinder.

NOTES — ABOUT GINGER

1. The words of seventeenth-century herbalist Culpeper.
2. The work is Rosemary Brissenden's *South East Asian Food* (Penguin, 1972), and I don't mean to sound ungrateful. Her comprehensive work often headed me in the right direction.
3. I came to realize after consulting several authorities that there is vast confusion about galangals and their botanical names. Both *A. galanga* and *K. alpinia* qualified as galingale in England. So did one *Alpinia officinarum*, which may or may not differ from the other two. As best I could determine, the most popular of the small, lesser galangals is *Kaempferia pandurata*.
4. Here too, the taxonomy gets tricky because some of the Zingiberaceae have been classified by their rhizomes as well as their seed pods. Black cardamom has been variously classified as *Zingiber nigrum*, *Alpinia allughas*, and, sometimes, *Amomum amarum*.
5. Ginger's piquancy as a dried spice and its predominance in English foods, beverages, and medicines bear major responsibility for linking the word spice to any ingredient that tastes hot. When Sichuan/Hunan cuisines first woke up people's taste buds on these shores, food writers constantly referred to the spiciness of these dishes, when in fact they aren't spicy at all. In this book I have included a quintessential Sichuan home-style fish dish with enough fresh ginger, garlic, fresh chili peppers, and fresh chile paste with garlic to give the ironhearted pause, but it hasn't a spice in it. (See p. 60.)
6. Gerard's description in 1597 was not new. Literature sent to me by the Australian Trade Commission about their ginger growing and processing industry cites a "fourteenth century sex manual," *The Perfumed Garden*, which advised, "A man who prepared himself for love with ginger and honey would give such pleasure to the woman that she would wish the act to continue forever."
7. The French word is *rase*, recognized in English also, from *racine* (root).
8. I should also mention the word "sauce," from which we get saucy, sauciness, sass, and sassy. Sauce originally meant just the spices added to food to give it life and came from the French *sallere* (to salt). A seventeenth-century recipe might instruct, "Add no sauce but salt," meaning leave out the ginger for once.
9. Contrary to many articles about ginger, *Jamaica* does not commercially export fresh ginger to the U.S., a fact verified by their trade commissioner in New York. And *Puerto Rico*, if it does ship it, is not much of a factor in the market since Puerto Rico was not mentioned by the major importers I talked to.

II.
THE
COOK'S
TOUR

EAST
TO
WEST

Tips For The Cook

The following recipes span the world and are in the style of their native lands as best I could make them. Some of the recipes may seem alien or complex to cooks who are not familiar with a particular cuisine, but I did avoid the more elaborate preparations of the ginger-using countries. This was a painful decision in the case of B'steeya, for example, since this Moroccan dish is famous, and ginger is an important flavor. The recipes should serve as an introduction to the authentic tastes of the chosen cuisines, and I hope the reader will pursue the favored ones in depth. For the people about to plunge in, I offer this advice:

Staples: Garlic, Chili Peppers, Coriander, and Others

Besides the special ingredients which are outlined in the section that follows, I found four seasonings that are used in abundance in all ginger-loving lands, and an appreciation of them will enhance the enjoyment of many of the recipes in this book. (By coincidence I am addicted to these flavors.) Foremost is garlic. With the exception of Japan and certain Indian sects, garlic is uninhibitedly used wherever there is ginger—particularly fresh ginger. Second is the chili pepper, fresh or dried, in pastes or in oils. A close third is coriander, which in its fresh form is the most popular herb on the planet. Fourth, and not quite so prevalent, is the cumin seed. Two others that surprised me with their worldwide importance are the coconut, a daily staple in tropical Asia, Africa, the West Indies, and Latin America, and the peanut.

Other than the information in the section Special Ingredients about chili peppers, I should caution that when handling fresh ones, be careful of the seeds and membranes which contain the fiery oils. Do not rub your eyes or elsewhere after preparing them. The best washing solution for your fingers is heavily salted water. Fresh coriander is best kept refrigerated with its roots in water and its leaves loosely covered by a plastic bag.

Salting and Seasoning

I would like to stress that the quantities of salt, pepper, chili peppers, spices, and even ginger listed in the recipes are suggested amounts, and reflect the taste of the author. The reader may adjust these according to taste. I should also point out that the recipes were tested using coarse Kosher salt, which is less salty than regular salt by nearly half. Kosher salt, I find, is more pleasant to cook with, particularly when sprinkling over meats, and its taste is less biting.

Utensils

No recipe requires unusual, expensive, or hard-to-get tools. I cook in a kitchen noticeably free of gadgets. Helpful, but not absolutely necessary, are the following:

- A 16-inch wok of tempered steel or cast iron, which I find useful for all cuisines, especially with whole poultry or fish. It is also the most efficient deep-frying pan. Accessories should include the lid, spatula, and skimmer for deep-frying. A large cast-iron skillet may substitute in most recipes.

- The inexpensive Chinese "sandy pot" (clay pot) casseroles, which come in all sizes, adapt themselves well to Indian and Moroccan cooking. They are flameproof, though the first few times they are to be used they must be immersed for an hour in water prior to cooking.

- The granite mortar and pestle, found where Asian cookware is sold, is the finest device I know of for crushing spices and herbs. They are Southeast Asian in origin, and are far more effective than their porcelain or wooden counterparts in meeting the demands of Southern Asian or Middle Eastern cooking. They are far cheaper than marble, I might add.

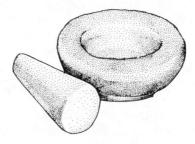

- It goes without saying that a kitchen should be equipped with razor-sharp knives, but a French chef's knife or an all-purpose (number 2) Chinese cleaver is particularly helpful.

- The Japanese ginger grater is discussed in the section Preparing Fresh Ginger (page 35).

Special Ingredients

L ike fresh ginger, most of these "special ingredients" are increasingly less special and more familiar to American cooks. The following guide should prove useful even to those who are acquainted with the foods on the list.

Bamboo Shoots. Buy canned whole bamboo shoots, which are found in Asian grocery stores, not the pre-sliced and canned ones found in supermarkets. Winter bamboo shoots are the best, but about twice the price. Campanion brand packs these in a large blue can. Ma Ling is another trustworthy name for plain bamboo shoots. Bamboo shoots should be boiled for 30 seconds and run under cold water before using in order to remove the tinned taste. Leftovers may be stored in the refrigerator, covered in water, for a week or so if the water is changed every other day.

Banana Leaves. Large fresh banana leaves are available refrigerated in plastic packages in Asian markets. They are moistened and ready to cut to size and stuff with any of a variety of mixtures for grilling, boiling, or steaming.

Basil (Asian). Asian or Thai basil can be found fresh in Southeast Asian produce markets. Whether green (*Ocimum canum*) or purplish (*O. sanctum*), it has smaller leaves than the variety familiar to Westerners (*O. basilicum*). The flower buds are similar, and you should be able to recognize these plants. Western basil is perfectly acceptable as a substitute.

Bean Sauce. Known in ancient China as "pickled beans," this salty, strong-flavored whole bean condiment was the original liquid from which soy sauce was later extracted. Bean sauce is used more in northern and western Chinese cooking than southern (and it should not be confused with the fermented black beans of the south).

Black Beans (Salted and Fermented). These make a wonderful seasoning that has a wine taste and is used in southern Chinese cooking. The beans come in plastic packages with bits of ginger and orange peel. Do not bother rinsing them; after lightly chopping, just soak them in *Shao hsing* or dry sherry. Toss them along with the wine into the dish when called for.

Black Mushrooms (Shiitake). A staple throughout East Asia, this mushroom's popularity is rapidly growing in the United States. There is a mistaken belief that fresh shiitake mushrooms, now grown here commercially, are better than the dried. Indeed they are a flavorful and meaty alternative to our cultivated mushrooms, but the more expensive dried varieties, with their thick, white-veined, cracked caps, have far more flavor. The best dried mushrooms are sold in well-appointed Chinese apothecaries, and are carefully graded. To use dried mushrooms, cover them with boiling water and allow to soak for at least a half hour. Drain and squeeze the mushrooms (saving the stock for another purpose), and rub them with sesame oil or freshly rendered fat before using.

Black Vinegar (Sweetened). This full-flavored vinegar tastes vaguely like Worcestershire sauce. It is packaged in 21-ounce bottles like soy sauce, and can be found on the same shelf in Chinese groceries. The best, aged variety comes in large crocks. It is prized for its cooling medicinal powers. There is also an unsweetened version.

Celery Cabbage (Chinese Cabbage). A staple of all East Asia, the squat, pale-green to white variety, often labeled "Napa," is best. Heads weigh up to 5 pounds and keep well in the vegetable crisper.

Cellophane Noodles (Chinese Vermicelli or Peastarch Noodles). These brittle, thin, nearly transparent noodles are wrapped and packaged in portions from 2 to 8 ounces. They are made from the flour of the mung pea, which when watered produces the popular bean sprout. The noodles are of Chinese origin, but are particularly popular in Southeast Asia.

Chili Paste with Garlic. An overwhelming variety of chili pastes are used in Asian cooking. The best of the Chinese brands is Lan Chi from Taiwan, which comes in an 8-ounce jar with a green label. It contains minced fresh garlic rather than powdered, and is full flavored and hot. The Vietnamese and Thai chili pastes now prevalent in Asian groceries are delicious but absolutely incendiary.

Chili Peppers (Dried). These peppers, no more than 2 inches in length, are sold in Asian and Indian grocery stores in plastic packages, and in some local food markets. They may be used whole when called for in a recipe, or powdered when a dish requires cayenne. Sichuan cooking demands that they be blackened in the cooking oil before proceeding with a dish.

Chili Oil. This is a fiery oil made from cooking ground, dried red chilis in oil, then straining it. Some chili oils include other seasonings. The Southeast Asian *Sa-te* oil is the hottest. Use it in dipping sauces with vinegar and soy sauce, or dribble it on a dish just before serving.

Coconut Milk. This is not the liquid inside the coconut, but the liquid blended with the meat. Quality coconut milk is now available in Asian markets in 8- and 14-ounce cans. Chaokoh from Thailand is one of many acceptable brands. To make your own: puncture two of the eyes of a husked coconut and drain the liquid into a container and set aside. Bake the coconut in a 375°F oven for 15 minutes, then split the shell with a hammer. The meat should fall away from the shell. (Stubborn pieces may be pried loose with a knife.) Pare the brown skin off of the coconut meat and blend the pieces with the liquid to make the milk.

Dashi. The essential stock in Japanese cuisine, this soup and sauce base is made from shavings of dried bonito (a fish of the tuna/mackerel family) and kelp. Purists shave their own petrified fillets with a special tool, and indeed it makes a difference; millions of Japanese, and most Japanese restaurants here, rely on *hon-dashi* (dried *dashi* granules), which makes an excellent broth. Dried bonito in fillets or flakes, or instant *dashi* mixtures are available in stores that carry Japanese foodstuffs. Make *dashi* fresh each time you use it as its flavor deteriorates rapidly.

Dried Shrimp. These tiny crustaceans are an important ingredient in Asia, West Africa, and Brazil. In this country they are most readily available at Asian groceries, where they are sold in plastic packages. Look for those pink in color and carefully cleaned. They will keep indefinitely in a sealed container away from heat and moisture.

Fermented Red Bean Curd. This is about the closest the Chinese come to a cheese. This powerful, salty Gorgonzola-like bean curd is used in meat dishes for color as well as flavor. The red comes from red rice, an expensive natural coloring. It is also known as wet bean curd. The best comes in small crocks, although it is available canned. Refrigerated in its crock, it keeps forever. Transfer canned curd to a jar for storage.

Fermented Sweet Rice (Wine Rice). This sweet, liqueur-like concoction with an intoxicating kick is used in northern and western Chinese cooking. Look for rice grains suspended in clear liquid in a plain jar found in the refrigerated sections of Chinese food stores that specialize in northern Chinese staples, particularly those from Shanghai. The English label is often misleading, particularly in states like New York where it is not legal to sell anything alcoholic in regular grocery stores.

Fish Sauce. This is the ubiquitous sauce of Southeast Asia, where it takes the place of soy sauce. Known as *nuoc mam* in Vietnam, *nam pla* in Thailand, and *tuk trey* in Kampuchea, this rotted fish extract tastes far more agreeable than its smell promises. The top quality variety, made from anchovies, is used for dipping sauce as well as for cooking. Fish sauce is highly nutritious; *nuoc mam* and rice were the K-rations that sustained the Viet Cong.

Five-spice Powder. It is not always the same five spices. Sometimes there are six in this Chinese blend, used mostly in the South for seasoning roasted meats or poultry. The most common spices are star anise, fennel seed, cinnamon, cloves, licorice root, fagara, and ginger.

Garam Masala. Simply called hot spices in some Indian English-language cookbooks, this North Indian blend is usually lightly roasted in a dry skillet and then added to taste while the dish is cooking. It can be purchased in Indian food stores, or you can grind it yourself in small quantities before using. Any excess can be kept in a tightly sealed jar away from light. To make about one-quarter cup: in a small coffee or spice grinder, grind 1 teaspoon cardamom seeds, 1 small cinnamon stick, 1 tablespoon cumin seeds, 1 tablespoon coriander seeds, 2 teaspoons of black peppercorns, and 6 cloves.

Hoisin Sauce. This thick, spiced soy paste is used in marinades for meats and as a sauce ingredient in North China. The sweetened varieties have proved popular with American eaters, and Hoisin sauce is always served with Peking Duck in this country.

Lemon Grass. The stalks of this grass, which is fundamental to Southeast Asian cuisines, look like stiff, light-green scallions. They are thinly sliced or bruised, then added to soups and sauces, or they are pounded with other seasonings to make the region's distinctive curry pastes. Now grown in the United States, lemon grass is available in markets selling Southeast Asian foods, and in well-stocked produce markets.

Mirin. This Japanese sweetened sake is used almost exclusively for cooking. It is often used instead of sugar and many brands are displayed on the shelves in Japanese or Korean groceries.

Olives. For the Moroccan recipes that require olives, avoid bland domestic varieties. Purchase the green, tan, or purple-brown olives available at Middle Eastern, Greek, or Italian food shops. Paula Wolfert recommends Italian Gaetas, Greek Kalamatas, or Greek Royal-Victorias.

Oyster Sauce. This exotic, thick southern Chinese sauce made from oysters and salt should, when cooked with onions, recall our first encounters with "chow mein" and "chop suey." As a rule, the more expensive, the better. The top grades, which are full of the essence of plump oysters, are used for dipping. And be thankful for the caramel coloring—its undoctored grey coloring is none too appetizing.

Paprika. This ground mild capsicum is sometimes called Hungarian pepper or Spanish pepper because of its importance in those cuisines. It is also a staple spice in Morocco. Look for Spanish varieties that are fragrant and bright red; with age it loses power and browns.

Preserved Lemons. If you plan to do any Moroccan cooking, these are essential and easy to make. There is no adequate substitute. Visitors to my kitchen often ask about the gallon jar of them I keep among my soy sauces, rice wines, and Asian vinegars. To make one gallon: sprinkle coarse salt over the bottom of a sterile gallon jar. Take three dozen lemons and quarter them lengthwise, leaving enough at the stalk end so the quarters are still joined. Sprinkle the flesh liberally with salt, and add them to the jar, pressing down firmly on each to release some juice and fill the space. Add some peppercorns, a stick of cinnamon, and a few dried chili peppers. When almost filled, take the lemons that won't fit and squeeze their juice over the lemons in the jar until they are completely covered with brine. Moroccans add a clean stone to weigh them down. Allow to mellow for a month. They may be kept unrefrigerated.

Rice Vinegar. This usually refers to the pale white vinegar found in Chinese and Japanese food stores. The popular Japanese varieties such as Marukan are milder than Western white vinegars and have a pleasant, slightly sweet flavor.

Rock Sugar, Chinese (Yellow Rock Sugar). These large amber crystals are a combination of raw brown sugar, honey, and granulated sugar, which produces the desired sheen and flavor in northern Chinese red-cooked dishes. They are available in 1-pound plastic packages or boxes. Granulated white sugar may be substituted in slightly smaller quantities.

Saffron. These dried stigmas are plucked in threes from each saffron crocus to make the world's most precious spice. You would hardly notice them if you had thousands of them in your pocket. Fortunately, a little goes far, and only a pinch is needed to dramatically flavor and color a dish. Before adding, saffron should be soaked in a couple of tablespoons of hot water for 15 minutes, and added with the water. Buy the threads; the powdered form, like most spices, deteriorates over time and is easily adulterated—not uncommon considering its cost per ounce.

Sansho (Japanese Pepper). The Japanese may be the only people on earth who do not traditionally use the common black (or white) peppercorn, *Piper nigrum*. Instead, they are the only ones who use the dried orange berry of an indigenous ash, related to the Sichuan peppercorn but not the same, as many authorities claim. Ground *sansho* is available in Japanese food stores.

Sesame Seed Oil. A contender for the world's most seductively flavored oil, this seasoning is fundamental to the cuisines of China and Japan. Like the Chinese sesame paste, the oil is pressed from roasted seeds. Cooking with it is a waste, since it loses its flavor over high heat and is expensive. Avoid sesame oil packaged in the new plastic squeeze bottles, as it tends to go rancid (after all, you wouldn't buy olive oil in plastic containers). I prefer the Japanese brand, Kadoya.

Sesame Seed Paste. Unlike the Middle Eastern tahini, this Chinese paste is made from roasted, rather than raw, sesame seeds. Lan Chi packages a good paste in an 8-ounce jar. This flavorful peanut butter-like sauce is used mostly in sauces for cold dishes or salads, and occasionally in marinades.

Seven-spices (Shichimi). Seven-flavors would be more accurate, since this Japanese mixture contains only two spices, *sansho* (see above) and ground dried chilis. The other ingredients are flakes of dried orange peel, white poppy seeds, sesame seeds, black hemp seeds, and bits of seaweed. This concoction is sprinkled over, or served with, a variety of dishes.

Shao Hsing Rice Wine. This fine, strong rice wine is used in Chinese cooking. It is deep golden, like the color of Scotch. The Taiwanese market a fine version with a striking red label. Better yet, buy the brand Hua Tiao Chiew from Zheijiang, China, where the wine originated. The blue label, the least expensive of three, is recommended for cooking. The only substitute is a good dry sherry. Substituting sake is akin to substituting a white table wine.

Sichuan Peppercorns (fagara, wild pepper). This is one of the oldest Chinese seasonings, and one of the few true spices in the cuisine. The name is confusing; its use is not limited to Sichuan, and it is not related to the black peppercorn. Nor does it "smite you with a heatwave" as Waverly Root proclaimed. It is not hot, but rather strangely numbing. It is available in Chinese food stores in plastic packages, and should be toasted to smoking in a dry skillet and ground in a mortar before using.

Tamarind. The pulp of a pod used as a souring agent throughout the tropics, it probably originated in Southeast Asia and southern India. You can buy the pods themselves, which look like large light-brown bean pods, or, more conveniently, you can buy the pulp in small blocks in Indian, Southeast Asian, and Latin American markets. Soak the amount of the pulp called for in enough hot water to cover for 30 minutes, then strain the liquid into the dish. The solid matter should be rubbed on the strainer to extract all that is flavorful. Blocks of tamarind pulp keep indefinitely unrefrigerated.

Water Chestnuts. Fresh ones are best, rather like coconut meat. The canned variety lose their sweetness and flavor. They are available fresh and canned at Chinese food stores. Fresh water chestnuts should be washed free of mud before peeling.

White Radish or Turnip (Daikon). This large, elongated white root is familiar to those who shop in Oriental produce markets. Daikon is a staple of both Chinese and Japanese cooking, and the Koreans have their own squat green version. The Chinese use it mainly for home-style stews, a few cold banquet dishes, and an occasional carved garnish. To the Japanese, it is integral to the highest art of their cuisine; they grate it with a special tool, shred, juice, or carve it for a wide variety of dishes.

GINGER
EAST TO WEST

ASIA: THE SOURCE

China

Southeast Asia

Japan and Korea

Ginger in China

. . . He was never without ginger when he ate. He did not eat much.
—From a guide to the exemplary habits of Confucius.[1]

I n 1972 in the Hunan Province, Chinese archaeologists made a spectacular discovery: Han Tomb Number 1, in which the body of the wife of the Marquis of Tai was found perfectly preserved after twenty-one centuries. Not only were her skin, muscles, and internal organs in remarkably good condition, but the essential foods of the time, which were buried in the tomb to nourish her after death, were also extremely well preserved. An adequate supply of fresh ginger was among the foodstuffs.

One might almost believe that the Chinese invented ginger. Three hundred years before the woman in the Han Tomb was born, it was a staple in the diet of Confucius, and most of its medicinal and culinary properties were common knowledge. A brief treatise, "Seeking the Root of Sapors," preserved in a third century B.C. philosophical compendium, suggests that the founding rulers of the Shang dynasty (eighteenth to twelfth century B.C.) were able to pinpoint a small region in Sichuan Province, hundreds of miles from their northern capital, where the finest ginger specimens were grown.[2] They looked upon this region much as wine connoisseurs in the West look with fondness to the Medoc district of Bordeaux.

Exactly when the rhizome was first cultivated may be impossible to determine. Like the farmyard pig (another ancient Chinese product), ginger is without a trace of a wild ancestor. Unlike the pig, which we know trotted around northern Chinese grain-farming communities in the sixth century B.C., ginger doesn't leave bones. We can only venture that pork with ginger was the first enduring Chinese combination, and that both were tossed in the first Chinese cooking vessel, the clay pot,[3] to be simmered in soup-stews called *kengs*.

Before pigs, there were wild animals to contend with. The earliest recorded use of ginger was in solutions for preserving venison, which also called for salt and cinnamon bark—a demonstration of the first culinary virtue attributed to both ginger and cinnamon. As the second century A.D. poet Chang Heng said, they "eliminate the stench of raw flesh."

51

Medicinal Origins

Ginger's importance today (Chinese cooking is unimaginable without it) is due as much to its medicinal properties as to its food value. When Chinese cuisine first evolved, there was not much distinction; most Chinese staples have a lengthy medicinal history. Americans now smack their lips over Hot and Sour Soup, but it is essentially an early doctor's prescription.[4] Tree ear mushrooms and dried lily buds, which add a delicate crunch and fragrance to the dish, were included origi-nally to improve circulation. Those who relish the taste of crisp, fresh water chestnuts might ponder their early use as binding agents for illnesses where high temperatures accompany diarrhea. Ginger's medicinal properties are discussed in GINGER AS MEDICINE, p. 167. Suffice it to say ginger was worshipped as a tonic when a food's healthful properties were an overriding concern.

Food for the Spirit

In China, ginger held importance beyond its medicinal value; it had spiritual significance. It was a means for communicating with the gods and a staple in sacrificial rites. Ginger was eaten during periods of abstinence when garlic and other seasonings were banned. Its earthly powers as a digestive aid and stomach purifier also included protect-ing the newborn. At the birth of a child a knob of ginger was tacked on the entryway of Chinese homes to absorb the harmful character traits of any visitors, a practice that has disappeared only recently. Ginger offerings are still attached to huge paper constructions during religious festivals in Hong Kong. These rhizomes fetch a good price when later auctioned by the sponsoring organizations. They are believed to increase fertility and ultimately lead to the birth of a son.

Ginger at the Foundation of the Cuisine

Ginger remained a primary ingredient in Chinese cooking when the pleasure of eating became a concern unto itself. Because its culinary properties were prized by the Chinese, fresh ginger was not relegated to the herbalist's shelf as were its cousins turmeric, cardamom, and galangal. During the Chou period (1200 to 221 B.C.) Chinese cooking as we know it emerged, and the rhizome became more important. The textures that distinguish Chinese food took on value. Ginger was not just tossed in a dish; it was sliced, shredded, or minced to complement the cut of the other ingredients. In fact, this sense of harmony was exemplified by Confucius, who was said to refuse food that was not properly cut. Chopsticks were adopted to pick up these pieces around this time—2,500 years before Europeans stopped using their hands.

Pasta and ginger were an item long before noodles knew tomatoes and basil. The Han culture (206 B.C. to A.D. 220) introduced the noodle to China, perhaps to mankind. The world's oldest surviving pasta dish may be the famous Beijing birthday noodle dish, Za Jiang Mein (page 69). The sauce, which includes minced pork, bean sauce, ginger, fagara peppercorns, and scallions, has hardly been tampered with for 2,000 years. The dish can be found in any restaurant featuring Beijing food, or in the homes of northern Chinese.

Ginger, bean sauce, fagara pepper, and salt were also used for curing meats and fish during the Han period, resulting in a kind of jerky which the upper classes kept handy for cocktail snacks. At the end of a feast, when the fresh food had run out, the guests had something to nibble on as they consumed large quantities of wine amidst acrobats and beautiful dancers. The feast may have included the likes of baked owl in peony sauce and shredded panther breast in swallow broth.

Cooking with Ginger: A Chinese Guide

China is a continent of cuisines, and changes in cooking took place regionally. Yet ginger remained a basic ingredient from the wheat cultures of the north to the rice cultures of the south. Its value to the Chinese is beyond curative powers or the notion that it builds *ch'i*, or spiritual life energy, like ginseng. In order to understand ginger's magic, one must appreciate its role when matched with the other ingredients in a dish.

Chinese cuisine puts fresh ginger to more varied, and I think better, use than does any other cuisine. The principles behind this use can to some extent serve as a guide to the use of the rhizome in any cuisine. Equally important, to understand how ginger is used helps to better understand Chinese cuisine.

Ginger as Yang. In the Chinese model of harmony, ginger is a yang, or hot ingredient. This is not just a metaphorical characterization. Ginger is quite pungent when you take a bit of it, and produces a warming sensation when swallowed. Ginger balances the cooling effects of yin foods in a dish. This concept of a well-balanced meal goes beyond simple nutrition, and for the Chinese is just as important to health. In the West we have not escaped this notion; we treat colds with warming fluids like chicken soup. However, it is not a concept we apply to everyday foods as the Chinese do.

Cooking methods are also categorized as yin or yang. Those that use water are more cooling than those that use oil. For example, simple poaching produces more yin foods than deep-frying, a yang method. A ginger dipping sauce is invariably served with poached chicken to balance its lack of heat.

People themselves may have yin conditions that require heavily gingered foods. When a woman has just given birth, she is in an extreme yin state.* The Cantonese long ago devised an intriguing post-partum pigs' feet stew which contains an astonishing quantity of ginger (some one and a half pounds of fresh chunks to three pounds of feet; see page 68). The pigs' feet are warm and nourishing, and add a gelatinous quality to the sauce that holds in the heat as it passes through the system. The base is a dark vinegar which balances the richness, and is an important cleansing agent and restorative.

Fish and Shellfish. The Chinese consider ginger a de-fisher, meaning it suppresses any hint of fishiness in even the freshest fish. The first time I found a chunk of ginger and a scallion in the bag when I bought a whole fish in New York's Chinatown, I thought it was a mistake, but it kept happening. Ginger and scallions (also a de-fisher) automatically accompany fish in the Chinese view, as if they were planted on earth for that purpose. Although Chinese seafood dishes of any sort are rare without ginger, crab is never served without it. Besides the wonderful flavor combination, crabmeat is considered the most cooling food.

Meat and Poultry. Ginger suppresses any hint of rankness in meat, game, and the myriad innards enjoyed by the Chinese. Since beef is not especially favored by the Chinese, it may get an extra heavy dose of ginger. However, the much-favored pork kidney gets the same treatment, being commonly served with thick slices of ginger. The use of ginger with chicken is routine, though not imperative. However, ginger is used in cooking ducks and geese to counteract any gaminess. If the bird is cooked whole, a chunk or two is skewered into the cavity or added to the cooking liquid.

The Chinese eschew the use of aromatic vegetables (carrots, celery,

---

* She is drained of *ch'i* (life energy); her blood count is low; her circulation is poor; her menstrual cycle has been disrupted; she is subject to chills. Her nursing requires that she have extra nourishment.

onions) to make stock, believing they take out more flavor than they add, and prefer just meat and bones (usually chicken), to which a piece of ginger is occasionally added.

Vegetable Cookery. It is no secret that the Chinese like fresh vegetables that are lightly cooked to maintain their crispness, color and nutritional value—a style referred to in a 1934 New York restaurant guide as "partially cooked greens." Today this light treatment is emulated in the West, even taken a step beyond with our passion for salads and raw vegetables—a step too far for Chinese enjoyment.

Ginger is used in Chinese vegetable dishes to rid them of their raw taste. It is used with all vegetables, but most commonly with the earthy cabbage family, which is integral to the Chinese diet. Various broccolis, bok choys, celery cabbages, round cabbages, and kohlrabi are rendered delicious with a light mince or a few shreds of ginger. For the same reasons, ginger goes well with mustard greens and root vegetables. Pickling vegetables with ginger or pickling the rhizome itself is common in the Chinese kitchen.

Ginger and Garlic: Ancient Harmony. The balance of ginger and garlic, another combination that seems part of some grand design, has been perfected over the centuries throughout China. Ginger refreshes odoriferous garlic, and garlic's mustiness in turn softens ginger's medicinal overtones. Together, they can be used in astounding quantities; in Sichuan country cooking, both explode with wonderful flavor as they work off one another. Using six or eight garlic cloves is not uncommon in a small dish, when balanced by a substantial portion of ginger.

Ginger and the Five Flavors. Early on, the Chinese picked out five flavors to juxtapose like musical notes in their cooking: sweet, sour, salty, bitter, and pungent. Ginger, the epitome of a hot (pungent) aromatic, readily works with all the others, and, if necessary, mitigates their excess: a heavy hand with salt can be corrected with a little fresh ginger. For the Cantonese, the Bitter Melon loses some of its appeal without ginger. Little else that is pungent goes so well with sweet food.

Ginger and Fats. A slice or two of ginger provides a refreshing flavor counterpoint to the rich, northern Chinese "red-cooked" casseroles. Minced with minced pork, it gives a lighter touch to the savory boiled, steamed, or pan-fried dumplings (*jao-tze*) particular to the same area. Furthermore, the Chinese feel that a little ginger is a big help when digesting anything rich.

Ginger as a Texture. The Chinese palate is perhaps the most finely attuned to how food feels in the mouth. The cut of the ingredients is almost as important as the ingredients themselves in determining the worth of a dish. Whether meat is hand chopped or ground in a machine might make little difference to a dish's acceptance in the West; but to the Chinese it is the difference between something to be enjoyed, maybe even to be honored by, and something run-of-the-mill. Ginger, above all seasonings, can be cut into either crisp slivers for a shredded dish, or fine hairs as a textural counterpoint to a delicate fish. Sharp bits of minced ginger, hand chopped of course, dramatize the texture of a pork stuffing. The textural value of ginger helped to solidify its culinary position around the first millenium B.C.

Ginger as a Spice. The Chinese cook only with the fresh rhizome, with two exceptions. Chinese along the southern coast enjoy the curries of their neighbors, and occasionally incorporate preblended powders or pastes, which include dried ginger, into their cooking. The other, more distinctly Chinese exception is a powder referred to as five-spice powder (see page 46). Roasted Cantonese spareribs, pork strips, ducks, and whole young pigs that are a familiar sight in Chinatowns throughout the United States are often seasoned with this mixture. These powdered spices are also used for preserving fruits, even ginger.

NOTES — CHINA

1. CONFUCIAN ANALECTS, trans. Legge, 1893, from *Food in Chinese Culture*. According to the ancient Analects, which guided the practitioners of Confucianism, ginger was such an important food that Confucius approved of its use even during periods of fasting or sacrificial worship, when the consumption of all other pungent or malodorous foods was prohibited.
2. From *Lu Shih Ch'un Ch'iu (Spring and Autumn of Master Lu)* provided by Don Harper of the Department of Oriental Languages, U.C. Berkeley, who recently researched the original work.
3. Clay pots (also known as "sandy pots") surprisingly similar to their ancestors are readily available in stores specializing in Chinese cookware. As pottery they are unusual in their ability to withstand direct flame—necessary a few thousand years ago.
4. Ingredients traditionally include: stock (usually chicken), bean curd, chicken blood, tree ear mushrooms, dried black mushrooms, lily buds, bamboo shoots, eggs, vinegar, soy sauce, sesame oil, white pepper, and sometimes meat. The dish, however, has wide variations.

Three Steamed Fish

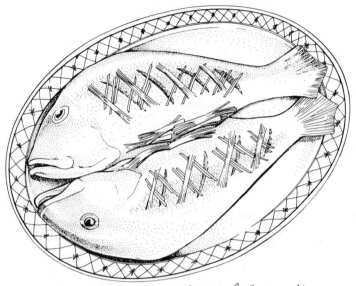

Steamed Fish – Guangzhou

There is no more perfect method to cook fish than steaming them whole in the Chinese manner. Sauces run the gamut from the simple garnishes of the south to near Western-style brown sauces and even pork sauces of the northern and western provinces. Ginger and scallions are the common denominator regardless of where they are cooked.

The first step in cooking fish anywhere in China is to start with a live one. In Hong Kong, Cantonese restaurants upon order scoop the fish from an aerated tank and bring it flapping to the customer's table for inspection—obviously not to check that the eyes are clear and the gills red (criteria in the West for how long ago it died), but to see just how alive it is. No Chinese gourmet, however famished, would eat a listless fish.

It is possible here to find live fish in tanks if you live near a Chinese market, though the choices are far more limited than in Asia. The following recipes work well with any absolutely fresh white-fleshed fish, even a dead one. On the West Coast this means top-grade rockfish or rock cod; on the East Coast sea bass or red snapper are a delicious choice. On both coasts flounder is excellent with lighter sauces.

Important Note: The following recipes, and all the recipes that call for whole fish in this book, specify the weight of the fish as it comes out of the water. Have your fishmonger scale and clean the fish for you; and make sure the head is left on.

STEAMED FISH NO. 1 • *Guangzhou*

One of the world's finest methods of cooking a whole fish is simply to steam it with fresh ginger, scallions, and wine as the Cantonese do. For this dish and the two that follow you will need a heat-proof platter and a steamer large enough for this platter with a fish on it. I recommend a large wok, 16 to 18 inches, fitted with a pie rack, and a large cover.

1 very fresh, whole white-fleshed fish, 1½ pounds (top-grade rockfish on West Coast, sea bass on East Coast)

1 teaspoon salt

2 teaspoons light soy sauce

1 tablespoon Shao hsing or dry sherry

1½ tablespoons peanut or vegetable oil

Pinch of sugar

1 tablespoon finely shredded fresh ginger

2 scallions, including the greens, shredded and cut into 2-inch lengths

Sprigs of fresh coriander for garnish

Rinse the fish and dry thoroughly. Score it lightly at 1-inch intervals with a sharp knife, and rub the salt over the entire fish. Combine the soy sauce, wine, oil, and sugar, and set aside.

Pour enough water into your steamer or wok to come to within an inch of the cooking rack. Cover and bring to a boil. Put the fish on a heat-proof serving platter, pour the sauce over it, decorate with the ginger and scallion shreds, and steam for 12 to 15 minutes or until the fish is just firm to the touch. Serve garnished with the coriander. The natural sauce is delicious. *Serves 2-4.*

STEAMED FISH NO. 2 • *Shanghai*

This more elaborate version of the simple steamed fish uses ginger as both a seasoning and a vegetable. It requires that a light sauce be made on the side and poured over the fish—a method borrowed by France's *nouvelle cuisine*.

4 dried black mushrooms

¼ cup finely shredded ginger

¼ cup finely shredded bamboo shoots

1 white-fleshed fish, 2 to 3 pounds (flounder, sea bass, red snapper, or top-grade rock cod)

3 tablespoons Shao hsing or dry sherry

2 tablespoons light soy sauce

1 teaspoon sugar

½ teaspoon salt, or to taste

¼ pound pork scraps

6 cross-section slices from a thick knob of fresh ginger

3 scallions, cut into 2-inch lengths

7 tablespoons peanut or vegetable oil

½ teaspoon white pepper

Fresh coriander leaves for garnish

Pour boiling water over the mushrooms and let soak for 30 minutes. Drain and shred the mushrooms and combine them with the ginger and bamboo shoots. Set aside.

Rinse and dry the fish, and put it on a heat-proof platter. Start the water boiling to steam the fish. Meanwhile, blend the wine, soy sauce, sugar, and salt and set aside.

Spread the pork, ginger slices, and scallions over the fish and steam for 15 to 20 minutes, depending on size and thickness.

Right before the fish is finished, make the sauce in a skillet or small wok: heat the oil, add the vegetable and mushroom shreds, and stir for 2 minutes. Finally, add the liquid seasonings, bring to a boil, and turn off the heat.

When the fish is done, discard the pork, scallions, and ginger slices, and transfer to a warm serving platter. Pour the sauce over the fish, sprinkle with the white pepper, garnish with coriander, and serve. *Serves 4-6.*

STEAMED FISH NO. 3 • *Sichuan Home-Style*

You will not find this kind of Sichuan country sauce, with a half cup each of chopped ginger and chilis, in your neighborhood restaurant, even if your neighborhood is Manhattan or San Francisco. It is not as delicate as Steamed Fish No. 1, but it's good. The fermented rice (see Special Ingredients, p. 46) gives this dish an important kick. (See Steamed Fish No. 1 for steaming techniques.)

1 white-fleshed fish, 1¾ to 2¼ pounds
Shao hsing *or dry sherry*
¼ cup peanut or vegetable oil
½ pound ground pork
½ cup finely chopped ginger
3 tablespoons chopped garlic
½ cup chopped fresh chili peppers

1½ tablespoons chili paste with garlic
5 tablespoons bean sauce
¾ cup fermented rice
½ cup water or chicken stock
1 cup chopped scallions
Fresh coriander leaves for garnish

Rinse the fish with water; then dry, and rinse again with a small amount of wine. Heat a large amount of water to boiling in a steamer or wok. Put the fish on an oiled plate or platter, place inside the steamer, and cover. The fish should be done in 15 to 20 minutes depending on the weight and thickness.

Meanwhile, heat the oil in a large saucepan or skillet and cook the pork, stirring to break up the lumps, until the meat changes color. Add the ginger, garlic, and peppers, stirring. Add the chili paste and bean sauce and cook another minute. Add the fermented rice and continue to stir over high heat, then add the water. Turn the heat down slightly and cook, stirring occasionally, for another 8 minutes or so. Watch that the sauce doesn't become too dry. (It may be necessary to add more water during the cooking.)

When the fish is done, transfer it to a warm serving platter. Stir the scallions into the sauce and pour over the fish. Garnish with the coriander and serve. *Serves 4-6.*

STEAMED CRABS WITH GINGER
SAUCE • China

Crabmeat is one of the most purely yin or cooling foods in Chinese cookery. It is almost always served with ginger to create harmony. This sauce is a popular accompaniment to the renowned Shanghai water crab, a dark green, fresh-water species the size of a large Eastern blue crab.

Two methods of preparing these crabs are popular. In one method, called "drunken crabs," they are allowed to expire swimming in *Shao hsing* and salt, then cracked and eaten uncooked—a Chinese sashimi. For the other, they are steamed whole for 20 minutes, a method familiar to U.S. crab lovers. Either way, the cracked crab is dipped in this wonderful ginger-laden sweet vinegar and soy sauce. Once they try this, many people lose their affection for melted butter.

*2 or more Eastern blue crabs, or 1
    West Coast Dungeness crab per
    person*
Water
Salt

Sauce (for two):

*2 round tablespoons minced fresh
    ginger*
2 tablespoons light soy sauce
*¼ cup sweetened black vinegar**

Cover the live crabs in water with several tablespoons of salt for an hour, so they will rid themselves of any sand or mud. Meanwhile bring the water to a boil in a steamer large enough to hold the crabs. Transfer the crabs to the steamer, cover, and cook for 20 minutes. While the crabs are steaming, mix all the sauce ingredients and set it out in individual bowls. Serve the hot crabs on a platter with tools for cracking the claws and legs.

* If you can't get Chinese sweetened black vinegar, mix 2 tablespoons minced fresh ginger, 2½ tablespoons sugar, 2 tablespoons light soy sauce, and 2 tablespoons mild vinegar.

SQUID WITH BLACK BEANS, CHILIS, AND YOUNG GINGER • China

The arresting pale-skinned baby ginger that appears in the early summer in Chinese markets is mild enough to be used as a vegetable. Here, thin slices are a visual complement to squid, scored and cooked to look like tiny pinecones. Red chili slices add color and a flavorful tension with garlic and fermented black beans. Slightly sweetened wine binds it all.

1 pound small fresh squid

2 teaspoons fermented, salted black beans

4 garlic cloves, finely chopped

2 tablespoons Shao hsing or dry sherry

1 teaspoon sugar

Salt to taste

4 tablespoons peanut or vegetable oil

12 to 15 1-inch oval slices of red chili peppers*

3 scallions cut into 1½-inch lengths, green part included

12 to 15 slices of young ginger or, if unavailable, 12 paper-thin slices of regular ginger

Clean squid. Cut off tentacles and put in bowl. Split the squid with a knife, then lay the white body of the squid inside-up on a cutting board. Scrape lightly with a sharp knife. Holding the knife almost parallel to the squid, score the body with straight cuts about 1/4-inch apart. Be careful not to cut through the squid. Turn the squid 90 degrees and repeat, so that you have a diamond pattern. Cut the body into six more or less equal pieces and add to the bowl with the tentacles.

Parboil all the squid in a large pot of boiling water for 30 seconds, run under cold water to stop the cooking, drain, and set aside.

Chop the black beans very lightly, add to a small bowl with the garlic and 1 tablespoon of the wine, and set aside. Mix the remaining tablespoon of wine with the sugar and 1/2 to 1 teaspoon of salt. Set aside.

Heat the oil in a wok or skillet until very hot. Add the peppers, scallions, and ginger, and stir very briefly. Add the black bean mixture. Stir just until you get a whiff of the wonderfully pungent mixture. Add the squid, then the seasonings, and stir rapidly just until it is good and hot. Serve on a warm platter. *Serves 4.*

* To prepare the peppers, remove the top of the pepper, slit the side, and flatten it out; then carefully cut out the inside membrane and seeds. Cut to approximately the shape of the ginger slices.

SHRIMP AND PORK KIDNEY SALAD • China

The textures and tastes of this colorful, cold Sichuan dish are heightened by their contrasts: pork kidneys/shrimp; cool temperature/hot flavors. I particularly appreciate the ginger and white pepper combination, a Sichuan taste that is often overlooked. The sauce, with the addition of garlic, is common to other salads of the region such as hand-cut chicken or shredded pigs' ears.

6 pork kidneys
¾ pound medium shrimp
1½ teaspoons cornstarch
½ egg white
1 teaspoon Shao hsing or dry sherry
½ cup celery, thinly sliced at a 45°
    angle
2 tablespoons shredded ginger

Sauce:
1 tablespoon sesame oil
1 tablespoon chili oil
2 tablespoons light soy sauce
2 tablespoons rice vinegar
¼ teaspoon salt
1½ teaspoons sugar
1 teaspoon white pepper, freshly ground
    if possible

Cut the kidneys in two lengthwise. Remove the veins and fatty tissue inside and rinse thoroughly in cold water. Slice very thinly into pieces as uniform as possible. Soak the slices in cold water at least 4 hours, preferably overnight. Change the water from time to time.

Meanwhile shell and devein the shrimp. Cut in half lengthwise and toss with the cornstarch, egg white, and wine. Let sit in the refrigerator at least 30 minutes.

Bring 3 cups or so of water to the boil, pour in the shrimp, stirring to separate, and blanch for 30 seconds.* Remove and rinse under cold water. Drain.

Parboil the kidney slices in a similar manner. Drain thoroughly and add to the shrimp. Repeat the process with the celery and ginger.

Toss these ingredients with the sauce ingredients, and serve in a favorite shallow bowl. *Serves 4-6.*

* The shrimp may have to be blanched longer than 30 seconds depending on their size.

WHITE-COOKED CHICKEN WITH GINGER AND SCALLION SAUCE • China

This simple, ancient method of poaching chicken is akin to the Cantonese Steamed Fish No. 1 (see page 58) in its purity of flavor. It is highly recommended that a very fresh farm-raised chicken be used for this recipe rather than the small, commercial chickens common to supermarkets these days, since these lack flavor.

1 4-pound chicken
3 pieces fresh ginger, ½-inch thick
1 tablespoon sesame oil

Ginger Dipping Sauce:
3 tablespoons light soy sauce
½ teaspoon salt

½ teaspoon sugar
½ teaspoon freshly ground white pepper
1 tablespoon Shao hsing or dry sherry
8 tablespoons peanut or vegetable oil
¼ cup finely chopped fresh ginger
¼ cup finely chopped scallions, white part only

Place the chicken in a large pot, add water to cover, and add the ginger. Bring to a boil, turn the heat to medium-low, cover, and simmer for 10 minutes. Turn the heat off and allow the chicken to sit for 30 minutes. Remove the chicken from the liquid (the broth may be strained, reduced, and used for another purpose), and allow to sit while you prepare the dipping sauce.

Combine the light soy sauce, salt, sugar, pepper, and wine. Heat the oil in a small pan to hot but not smoking. Turn off the heat and add the ginger and scallions. Stir for 15 seconds, then add the sauce, and stir to combine. Set aside in small serving bowls.

Cut the chicken into serving pieces, then chop these into bite-size pieces, Chinese style. Arrange the pieces on a serving platter, and brush with the sesame oil. Serve accompanied by the dipping sauce. The chicken should be barely warm, the temperature at which the chicken will be most flavorful. *Serves 4-8.*

CHARCOAL-GRILLED DUCK WITH RED BEAN "CHEESE" • China

The Chinese often employ two or more methods when cooking a duck: for example, steaming with seasonings then deep-frying. The duck in this recipe is simmered with fresh ginger, wine, and scallions, then marinated in a rich paste pungent with bean sauce, five-spice powder, and fermented red bean curd, the closest the Chinese come to a cheese. When the duck is finally charcoal-grilled, the meat is unusually moist and permeated with flavor, and the skin has a smokey sweet crispness.

I first served this Chinese "cheese" dish to Laurie Chenel, whose California goat cheese has sparked an explosion of interest across the land. The dish was inspired by her visit to a recipe testing session.

1 4- to 5-pound duck	3 tablespoons light soy sauce
8 cups water	1 tablespoon bean sauce
3 1-inch chunks ginger	1 tablespoon sesame seed paste
2 scallions	1 teaspoon five-spice powder
¼ cup Shao hsing or dry sherry	4 tablespoons sugar
2 tablespoons fermented red bean curd	Peanut or vegetable oil

Remove the feet from the duck, if necessary. With kitchen shears or a heavy French chef's knife, cut along either side of the backbone and remove it along with the neck and head. Spread the duck flat and press to crack the rib bones so it will lie flat on the grill. Be careful not to puncture the skin.

Bring the water to a boil. Add the duck, ginger, scallions, and wine. Return to a boil and skim the surface as you would a stock. Simmer the duck for 45 minutes; then remove from the broth and set both aside.

Blend the bean curd, soy sauce, bean sauce, sesame seed paste, five-spice powder, and sugar with ¼ cup of the duck broth, skimmed right from the top to include some fat. Save the rest of the stock for another purpose. Rub the duck generously with the marinade, wrap it in foil and refrigerate until an hour before cooking. (Simmering and marinating may be done the night before.)

Preheat the grill over a moderate charcoal fire. Sear the skin side of the duck for about 5 minutes. Turn and cook 10 minutes, basting with a little oil or reserved marinade. Turn once more and cook for another 5 minutes to finish crisping the skin. Remove from the heat and let the duck rest for 5 minutes. Cut into Chinese-style bite-sized pieces or into quarters and serve. *Serves 4-8.*

LION'S HEAD WITH PINE NUTS • A Chinese Casserole

The world's most delicious (and rich) meatballs come from the Shanghai area. Fresh ginger takes the edge off the richness. Minced, fried pine nuts serve almost as a grain, enhancing a texture that melts in the mouth. Celery cabbage soaks up the wonderful flavors.

Chinese cookbooks printed here have adjusted the proportion of fat in Lion's Head for what they construe as American tastes; some even suggest that lean pork be used, ruining the dish. To understand its appeal is to make it authentically. Just cut down the amount that you eat . . . if you can.

2 cups peanut or vegetable oil for deep-frying, plus 2 tablespoons

1 cup pine nuts

1½ pounds hand-chopped, fresh uncured bacon (you may substitute coarsely ground fatty pork, though it is less authentic)

1 tablespoon cornstarch

1½ teaspoons salt, or to taste

3 tablespoons dark soy sauce

3 tablespoons Shao hsing *or dry sherry*

1 lightly beaten egg

1 tablespoon finely minced ginger

6 tablespoons water

3 pounds Chinese celery cabbage

1 tablespoon sugar

Heat the 2 cups of oil in a wok or skillet until hot. Turn off the heat and add the pine nuts. Remove them when they're lightly browned, taking care not to burn them. Chop the nuts and set aside.

Mix the pork with the cornstarch, 1 teaspoon salt, 1½ tablespoons dark soy sauce, 1 tablespoon wine, egg, ginger, pine nuts, and 2 tablespoons of the water. Stir in one direction with your hand until well blended. Wet your hands and make four slightly flat meatballs. Reheat the deep-frying oil and brown the meatballs, then drain. (This doesn't cook them, but merely seals their juices and gives them a pleasing crust.)

Wash the cabbage and set aside four outer leaves. Cut the rest into 2-inch strips and stir-fry in 2 tablespoons of oil until thoroughly wilted, 4 to 5 minutes. You'll need a large wok or skillet for this. Place the cooked cabbage on the bottom of a heat-proof casserole, and place the meatballs on top. Cover each one with the upper portion of a reserved cabbage leaf. Combine the remaining 4 tablespoons water, 2 tablespoons wine, 1½ tablespoons soy sauce, and ½ teaspoon salt with 1 tablespoon sugar and pour over the meatballs. Cover and simmer for 1 hour and 15 minutes. Serve in the casserole. The cooked cabbage-covered meatballs are said to resemble four little lion's heads. Maybe, with enough rice wine! *Serves 4-8.*

SHANGHAI-STYLE GINGER CARAMEL SPARERIBS • China

These small sparerib pieces, which make long golden threads of sweet and sour caramel when you pull them apart, could just as easily be in the confection section of this book.

3 to 3½ pounds pork spareribs (have the butcher cut across the bone into 1½-inch strips)
Oil for deep-frying
½ cup sugar

⅓ cup red wine vinegar
1 teaspoon salt
1 tablespoon dark soy sauce
3 tablespoons finely chopped ginger

Rinse the ribs in cold water, dry, and cut into separate pieces.

Heat the oil to very hot. Deep-fry the ribs until crispy brown, 5 to 8 minutes—this may have to be done in two batches. Drain.

Mix the sugar, vinegar, salt, and soy sauce, and set aside.

Remove the oil from the wok. Heat 1 tablespoon of oil and add the ginger. Stir-fry briefly then add the vinegar-sugar mixture. Cook over high heat until the sauce becomes syrupy. Add the ribs and stir rapidly until they're well coated. Remove to a lightly oiled platter. Serve warm or at room temperature. *Serves 6-8.*

PIGS' FEET WITH GINGER AND BLACK VINEGAR • China

This Cantonese dish is ritually shared with visitors to the household of a woman who has just given birth. It's eaten daily for at least a month from a pot that is kept simmering over a low flame. Fresh pigs' feet are added and the sauce is continually replenished, and grows ever richer and more nourishing. Besides the benefits of the other ingredients, it is felt that the dose of ginger to be had from this stew (which contains 1½ pounds) prevents the new mother from catching a chill, helps her reproductive cycle return to normal, and aids her digestion. But my experience has been that you don't have to have a baby to enjoy it.

3 pounds pigs' feet, split into 2-inch pieces by the butcher

1½ pounds peeled fresh ginger, cut into ½-inch chunks

21-ounce bottle Chinese sweetened black vinegar

½ tablespoon dark soy sauce

2 teaspoons salt, or to taste

Rinse the feet and put them in a heavy pot with water to cover. Bring this to a boil, then drain and rinse them well. Cover the pigs' feet with water, about 4 quarts, and bring to a boil again. Reduce the heat to medium, cover, and cook for 45 minutes.

Remove the cover. Add the ginger, vinegar, soy sauce, and salt. Reduce the heat and cook for another 2 hours, checking and stirring from time to time. There should be about 2 cups of slightly syrupy sauce at the end. *Serves 6-8*.

ZA JIANG MEIN—The World's Oldest Pasta Dish? • Beijing

This spaghetti with meat sauce can be traced to around 100 B.C. Although *jiang* is the Mandarin word for ginger, the *jiang* in the title of this dish refers to the bean sauce, literally bean pickle, which is a staple of northern and western Chinese cooking.

As with any ancient recipe, versions are nearly as numerous as the cooks who make it. The authentic versions, such as the one I've included below, tend to be somewhat salty and oily for Western tastes, but the Chinese intend that a little of this sauce go a long way compared to what a Westerner is used to. Adjust the oil and the bean sauce to taste. This dish is wonderful served with a platter of shredded garnishes such as sweet or hot peppers, carrots, cucumbers, celery, fresh coriander, or whole bean sprouts.

½ cup peanut or vegetable oil

1 pound ground pork, the fattier the better

¼ cup chopped ginger

6 tablespoons bean sauce

1 teaspoon Sichuan peppercorn powder

1½ teaspoons sugar

1 pound Chinese fresh noodles (mein)

1 teaspoon sesame oil

½ cup scallions, cut into ½-inch lengths

Heat the oil in a wok or heavy skillet and add the pork. Stir and mash the pork in the oil to break up any clumps. When the granules have separated, add the ginger and stir for 1 minute. Add the bean sauce, the peppercorn powder, and the sugar and stir until the sauce is bubbling hot. Turn off the heat while you prepare the noodles.

Bring 4 quarts of water to a boil in a large pot and add the noodles. Turn the heat down slightly, and stir the noodles with a large fork to make sure they're separated. Cook for just 3½ minutes. Drain in a colander. Dribble the sesame oil over the noodles and toss briefly. Reheat the sauce and stir in the scallions. Serve the sauce and the noodles separately, with any or all of the suggested garnishes. *Serves 4-6.*

REAL GINGER BEEF • China

"What on earth would the Chinese kitchen do without fresh ginger?" asks Craig Claiborne introducing this dish in his and Virginia Lee's *The Chinese Cookbook*.

Chinese restaurants and cookbooks, excepting the above, rarely offer more than an insipid version of this popular dish. The full cup of ginger combined with 2 cups of fresh coriander leaves produces a warm, buttery flavor, almost a sensation, that should prove excitingly new. Macerating the ginger in salt keeps the amount of it from overwhelming the dish, and it may be reduced according to taste; but try this first.

1 pound flank steak, sliced as thinly as possible across the grain

1 tablespoon cornstarch

1 tablespoon dark soy sauce

1 tablespoon sesame oil

½ teaspoon freshly ground white pepper

1 cup finely shredded ginger

1½ teaspoons salt, or to taste

1 teaspoon sugar

3 tablespoons Shao hsing *or dry sherry*

1 cup peanut or vegetable oil

2 cups fresh coriander leaves, lightly chopped and firmly packed

Marinate the beef in the cornstarch, soy sauce, sesame oil, and pepper for 30 minutes in the refrigerator.

Meanwhile, in a small bowl, toss the ginger with the salt and set aside for 20 minutes; then squeeze the shreds to extract most of their moisture, and set aside. Combine the sugar and wine and set aside.

When the beef has marinated, heat the oil in a wok or skillet to a warm-hot temperature. Add the meat, stirring to separate the pieces. When the pieces change color remove them to a colander to drain. (Some of the meat may still be pink.) Remove all but 3 tablespoons of the oil from the pan. (It may be strained and saved for another use.)

Heat the 3 tablespoons of oil in the pan and add the ginger. Stir rapidly for 15 seconds, add the beef, and cook stirring for another 15 seconds. Stir in the coriander leaves and the wine mixture, and cook just until the dish is heated through, and serve. *Serves 3-4.*

CELERY CABBAGE AND WHITE TURNIP SALAD • China

This buffet or banquet relish is another study in contrasts Sichuan-style. It is cool in temperature yet hot in taste with two-thirds cup of shredded ginger. It is sweet and sour, and it is a mound of crinkled shreds in shades of white with a dozen blackened chili peppers.

2 pounds celery cabbage (the stout white variety)
1 pound white radish (daikon)
Salt
3 tablespoons peanut or vegetable oil
2 tablespoons sesame oil

2 teaspoons Sichuan peppercorns
9 tablespoons sugar
6 tablespoons red wine vinegar
12 dried hot peppers
2/3 cup finely shredded ginger

Cut the cabbage into quarters lengthwise. Cut out the core and cut across the leaves into the finest possible shreds. Peel the radish, and slice into the thinnest possible rounds. Stack and shred these as finely as you can. Toss the cabbage and radish shreds in a large mixing bowl with 2 tablespoons of salt. Let the salted shreds sit for 1 hour or so; then transfer to a colander and squeeze out as much liquid as possible with your hands. Arrange the shreds on a platter while you prepare the sauce.

Combine the vegetable and sesame oils with Sichuan peppercorns in a wok or skillet and heat until the peppercorns blacken and begin to smoke.* Turn off heat, cover, and allow to cool. Meanwhile, in a saucepan, briefly heat the sugar, vinegar, and ½ teaspoon salt, cooking just until the salt and sugar dissolve.

Strain the seasoned oil into another pan and heat. Add the dried chili peppers. When they begin to blacken and smoke, add the ginger shreds and stir for 20 seconds, then add the vinegar mixture, bring to a boil, and turn off the heat. After it cools somewhat, pour the sauce over the cabbage and radish shreds and allow to reach room temperature. Toss lightly before serving. This is also delicious chilled, and it keeps for a week or so refrigerated before its texture deteriorates. Serves 4-8.

* Be sure your exhaust fan is on when blackening the seasonings.

ZUCCHINI WITH CARROTS AND GINGER SHREDS • China

A simply made vegetable dish that may be stir-fried and served warm, or made ahead of time and served room temperature as a salad.

1 pound small zucchinis
3 tablespoons peanut or vegetable oil
¾ cup shredded carrots
¼ cup shredded red bell pepper
1½ tablespoons finely shredded fresh
 ginger
1 teaspoon salt
Dash of white pepper
Few drops of sesame oil

Cut the zucchini in half lengthwise, then place the cut side down on the cutting board and cut lengthwise into thin slices. Cut the slices into 2-inch lengths.

Heat the oil in a wok or skillet until nearly smoking. Add the zucchini and cook, stirring 30 seconds. Add the carrot shreds, the pepper shreds, and the ginger and stir for another 15 seconds or so. Add the salt and pepper and continue to stir until the vegetables are slightly softened but crunchy. Turn off the heat, sprinkle with the sesame oil, and remove to a serving platter. *Serves 4-6.*

SICHUAN CUCUMBER PICKLE

Where I lived until recently, in a small upstate New York village, everyone canned the bounty from one's garden in the fall. Though I did not grow Chinese black mushrooms or Sichuan peppercorns, my cucumbers and hot peppers went into this piquant spiced mixture.

1 tablespoon light soy sauce

8 hot dried peppers

4 to 6 black mushrooms, soaked, squeezed, and shredded

2 tablespoons fresh ginger, shredded

4 to 6 red chili peppers, shredded

4 cucumbers (about 3 pounds)

2 tablespoons salt (coarse, if possible)

¼ cup peanut or vegetable oil

1 tablespoon Sichuan peppercorns

5 tablespoons sugar

5 tablespoons red wine vinegar

Cut off and discard ends of cucumbers. Cut in half lengthwise, then scrape away the seeds. Slice the cucumber pieces thinly into half moons and put them into a mixing bowl. Toss the slices with the salt and let sit for an hour.

Meanwhile heat the oil in a saucepan, add the peppercorns, and cook until they begin to blacken. Turn off the heat and let sit covered.

Combine the sugar, vinegar, and soy sauce. Strain the peppercorn-seasoned oil into a skillet or wok, add the dried peppers, and turn on the heat. When they begin to blacken and smoke, add the shredded mushrooms, ginger, and chili peppers. Stir briefly and rapidly in the oil, then add the sugar-soy-vinegar mixture. When it all comes to a boil, turn off the heat.

Squeeze as much water as possible from the salted cucumber slices and transfer to a bowl. Pour the warm liquid over the cucumbers and allow to cool.* Serve at room temperature or chilled. These will keep for a week in a jar in the refrigerator—probably longer, though they are always gone before then in my house. *Makes about 1½ pints (6-10 servings).*

* If canning, after you squeeze the water from the cucumbers and mix them with the sauce, put them in canning jars and follow directions for sterilizing that apply to any pickle.

PEARS IN HONEY WINE SAUCE • China

Pears with fresh ginger, poached in a honey and wine sauce, and spiced with cinnamon is a delicious way to end any meal. A touch of dark soy sauce adds a deep golden color and rounds out the flavor.

4 ripe, unblemished pears

1 lemon

1 cup water

5 1-inch lumps of Chinese golden rock sugar (or 5 rounded tablespoons of granulated sugar)

3 tablespoons honey (Chinese Lichee honey if you can get it)

1 2-inch cinnamon stick

6 thick slices of peeled fresh ginger

½ teaspoon dark soy sauce

½ cup Shao hsing (or dry sherry)

Cut the pears in quarters lengthwise. Core them, remove the stems, coat with the juice from half the lemon, and set aside.

Put all the rest of the ingredients, except the wine, in a large saucepan (don't forget the juice from the other half of the lemon), and bring to a boil. Add the wine and the pears and bring to a boil again. Simmer the pears over medium heat for 5 to 10 minutes until tender. Remove the pears and keep warm. Strain the sauce into a small skillet or other wide-bottomed pan that will enable you to reduce the sauce quickly. Turn the heat to high and reduce the sauce to a light syrup. Pour over the pears and serve. *Serves 4-6.*

Ginger in Southeast Asia

In the currency of the spirit world, ginger is gold.
—Laotian saying[1]

I t is not known whether the people of China or India introduced ginger to Southeast Asia centuries ago. It could very well be neither—perhaps it grew wild in these regions from the beginning. The climate is ideal for the ginger family; *Z. officinale* and its cousins are as intrinsic to the cuisines and the medicinal and spiritual concerns of Southeast Asian cultures as anywhere in Asia. Markets are filled not only with fresh ginger rhizomes in all stages of development, but several species of galangal and the fresh turmeric rhizome, called "yellow ginger."

Southeast Asian cultures have their own idiosyncratic uses for ginger, in addition to those shared with China and India. Fresh turmeric is more likely to be used than dried turmeric. The large galangal, *A. galanga*, claimed as native both in Thailand (where it is called "Siamese ginger") and Java (where it is called "Java root"), is often used to the exclusion of *Z. officinale*. Frequently two or three gingers are used in the same dish. A soup might typically include a slice of fresh galangal, a pinch of dried galangal ("laos powder"), turmeric, and fresh *Z. officinale*. Besides the rhizomes, Southeast Asian cooking calls for Zingiberaceae leaves (turmeric, especially, for wrapping meat or fish to be barbecued), and varieties of the seed pods or cardamoms. Even ginger flowers are eaten, although most, which are of blazing tropical brilliance, proliferate as ornamentals throughout the region.

As a broad generalization, Southeast Asian cuisines are an amalgam of ancient Chinese and Indian cooking styles. The ingredients draw on both, but add vital flavors that are uniquely Southeast Asian. Fresh basil, mint, and coriander are stir-fried Chinese style with ginger and garlic in Burma, Thailand, Vietnam, and Kampuchea. The ubiquitous fermented fish sauces take the place of soy sauce, and are balanced nicely by the refreshing tastes of ginger, mint, and lime. In the popular curry dishes associated with Indonesia and Malayasia, but characteristic of the whole region, ginger and its cousins are pounded in a mortar to a paste which is fried, then thinned with coconut milk before meat, fish, or vegetables are added. Lemon grass and thick malodorous shrimp pastes, which are indigenous to Southeast Asian cuisines, along with coriander seeds and chilis, are typically included.

The Chinese Influence

The wok is the utensil of choice throughout Southeast Asia. As in China, it is used for steaming and deep-frying, though most commonly for stir-frying. The translation of this most Chinese of cooking methods does not include the Chinese concern with the cut of the ingredients. Fresh ginger, sometimes minced or shredded, is usually simply added in slices the size of a coin. In Thailand or Laos this is just as likely to be fresh galangal.

The Indian Influence

Throughout Southeast Asia the first step of an exotic stew is a procedure of Indian influence: the pounding of spices with fresh seasonings into a paste which is then fried. The pastes may incorporate galangal as well as fresh ginger, or even fresh turmeric. Small finger-like galangals, called *krachai* in Thailand or *kentjur* (see p. 23) in Indonesia, may be shredded, or peeled and left whole to simmer with the other ingredients.

It should be noted that when Westerners think of curried dishes, they often conjure up food to which a standard powder (made yellow by turmeric) has been added as a seasoning. The cooks of Southeast Asia and India do not reach for a tired blend of ground spices, but roast and grind, as needed, only those spices which enhance the fresh ingredients of a particular dish. Curry is a genre of cooking rather than a flavoring.*

* I would encourage people to try the dishes labeled curries in fine Southeast Asian restaurants, since the spice blends will be markedly different from Indian ones. The curries most derivative of Indian cooking are called *Mussamen* (Muslim) or *Gaeng Mussaman* on Thai menus.

NOTES — SOUTHEAST ASIA

1. Ginger is one of the most important foods of the Lao *hon* (comparable to the Chinese yang) or heat-producing foods revered for their medicinal properties. Peppercorns and capsicum peppers are also *hon*, but ginger alone has ritual significance and is offered to the gods.

LIME-MINT DEEP-FRIED FISH · Thailand

This crispy fried whole fish swims upright in a sweet lime sauce that contains mushrooms, onions, and plenty of ginger. If you have the ingredients, the time, and a large enough wok, it's a wonderful centerpiece to a Southeast Asian or Chinese meal.

1 whole white-fleshed fish (rock cod, sea bass, or red snapper), about 3 pounds

2 eggs beaten

Salt

Cornstarch

5 dried black mushrooms

1 small onion, quartered

¼ to ½ cup thinly sliced ginger, preferably young

5 garlic cloves, crushed

4 small or 2 large red chili peppers, cubed

2 scallions cut into ½-inch lengths

1 ¾ cups reserved mushroom soaking liquid or water

½ cup white vinegar, preferably rice vinegar

¼ cup lime juice

1 tablespoon grated lime peel

¾ cup sugar

1 tablespoon dark soy sauce

2 tablespoons fish sauce

1 teaspoon salt

2 ½ tablespoons cornstarch

Peanut or vegetable oil

½ cup lightly packed mint leaves

Fresh coriander leaves for garnish

Cut fish lengthwise underneath head and stomach almost through to the back fin. Place stomach-side down on cutting board and press hard with the heel of your hand on the head of the fish to crack the bone (so the fish will remain upright). Score the fish at 1-inch intervals, but not through to the backbone.

Blend the eggs and 1 teaspoon salt, and rub all over the fish and into the scored surface.

Spoon a couple of tablespoons of cornstarch into a sieve and shake it over the fish. Rub it in well and let stand for 15 minutes. Repeat this 3 or 4 times.

Meanwhile, soak the dried mushrooms in a bowl of hot water for 20 minutes. Drain, reserving the liquid. Squeeze to extract the moisture, then cut off and discard the stems. Cut in thirds and add to a bowl with the onion quarters, ginger, garlic, peppers, and scallions.

Combine 1½ cups of the mushroom liquid or water with the vinegar, lime juice, lime peel, sugar, soy sauce, fish sauce, and salt. Heat in a small saucepan to blend. In a small bowl, mix the remaining ¼ cup soaking liquid with the 2½ tablespoons cornstarch and set aside.

Heat enough oil in a large wok to cover the fish. When near smoking (at least 375°F), cook the fish, spooning over the oil if necessary, for 8 to 10 minutes. Remove and drain.

Heat 3 tablespoons of oil in a wok or skillet to make the sauce. Add the vegetables and stir-fry 1 minute. Add the warm sauce and bring to a boil. Stir in the mint leaves. Stir the cornstarch again and add to the wok. When blended and thickened, turn off the heat.

Deep-fry the fish another 5 minutes until crispy brown; drain, and place on a large serving platter. Pour the sauce over the fish, garnish with the coriander leaves, and serve. *Serves 4-6.*

MALAY EEL CURRY · Malaysia

Finding fresh eels should not present a problem to those who like to fish, or who live near Asian markets, where they are kept live in tanks. If you purchase rather than catch them, have them cleaned, skinned, and cut into 1½-inch sections. The following is a wonderful way to enjoy them, especially if it is your first time.

1 or 2 eels (2 to 2½ pounds total)

Cornstarch

½ cup peanut or vegetable oil

3 tablespoons coriander seeds

1½ teaspoons fennel seeds

1½ teaspoons cumin seeds

6 to 8 dried chilis

2 teaspoons turmeric

2 teaspoons laos powder

1 1-inch cube fresh ginger, smashed

2 medium yellow onions, chopped

3 cloves garlic, peeled and smashed

2 stalks lemon grass, finely chopped

Small piece tamarind pulp, the size of a marble, softened in ¼ cup warm water

14-ounce can coconut milk

1½ teaspoons salt, or to taste

½ teaspoon freshly ground black pepper

Coriander leaves for garnish

Dredge the eel sections in cornstarch until they are lightly coated. Heat the oil in a heavy skillet or wok, brown the pieces, and set them aside.

Toast the coriander seeds, fennel seeds, cumin seeds, and chilis in a dry skillet just until fragrant. Add the turmeric and laos powder and continue to toast for a minute, taking care not to burn the spices.* Remove to a large mortar or blender. If using a mortar, pound the spices to a paste with the ginger, onions, garlic, and lemon grass, using half the cooking oil as a moistener. This may have to be done in batches. If using a blender, simply combine the toasted spices, ginger, onions, garlic, and lemon grass, and blend to a paste. Pour the tamarind water through a fine mesh strainer into a small bowl, mashing the pulp against the mesh to extract all the juice. Set aside.

Heat the remaining oil and add the paste. Stir and cook until the paste browns slightly, taking care it does not burn. Add the coconut milk, tamarind liquid, salt, and pepper, and bring to a boil. Reduce the heat to medium, and cook for 5 minutes, stirring occasionally. Add the eel pieces and cook for 10 minutes or so. Ideally the sauce should thicken and the oil start to separate when the fish is cooked. You may have to increase the heat if this has not happened; or if it is cooking too fast, add some water. Transfer to a serving dish and garnish with coriander. *Serves 4-6.*

---

* If you can get fresh galangal, add 3 thick slices to the sauce when you begin to cook it, and omit the laos powder. If you can get fresh turmeric, peel and add a 2-inch section to be pounded or blended with the rest of the ingredients into a paste, and forget the powder.

CHICKEN WITH MINT, BASIL, AND PEANUTS • *Thailand*

I find the fresh herb-ginger-chili combination of Thai cooking addicting, especially when bound with the contrasting flavors of fermented fish sauce and lime juice. In this example, which uses a Chinese cooking technique, deep-fried peanuts are sprinkled over at the end as a lavish garnish.

Chicken parts (1 whole breast, 1 leg with thigh, liver, gizzard, and heart)

1 egg white

1 tablespoon cornstarch

½ teaspoon salt

Peanut or vegetable oil

1 cup raw peanuts

8 small garlic cloves, smashed

8 ½-inch cubes of ginger, smashed

10 small or 5 large red chilis, seeded and cubed

6 scallions, white part only, cut into ½-inch lengths

⅓ cup fresh mint leaves

⅓ cup fresh basil leaves

⅓ cup fresh coriander leaves

Fresh coriander leaves for garnish

Sauce:

2 tablespoons freshly squeezed lime juice

2 tablespoons fish sauce

1 tablespoon light soy sauce

½ teaspoon salt

1½ tablespoons sugar

1 teaspoon Thai or Chinese chili paste with garlic

Skin and bone the chicken pieces. Cut the meat into cubes of less than ½-inch and put into a mixing bowl. Cube the liver and add to the bowl. Remove the membrane from the gizzard and cube. Score (crosshatch) the gizzard cubes and the heart and add to the bowl. Mix the chicken with the egg white, cornstarch, and salt, and refrigerate for at least 30 minutes.

Heat 1½ cups oil in a wok. When hot, turn off the heat and add the peanuts. Remove to a paper towel when they're light brown, and set aside. Leave the oil in the pan.

Combine the garlic, ginger, chilis, and scallions, set aside, and put the fresh herbs together. Blend the sauce ingredients. Reheat the 1½ cups oil and add the chicken pieces, stirring to separate. Cook for 2 minutes or until they change color, drain, and set aside. Drain the oil except for 2 tablespoons from the wok.

Turn the heat to high, then add the garlic, ginger, scallions, and chilis. Stir for 30 seconds. Add the sauce, then the chicken, and the fresh herbs. Cook over high heat until the liquid is mostly reduced. Remove to a serving platter. Sprinkle with the peanuts and the remaining coriander leaves. *Serves 3-4.*

GINGER FLOWER GRILLED IN BANANA LEAF
(Kanab Dok Khing) • Laos

Besides the ginger flower, Laotians use a number of exotic buds or floral hearts in their cooking, including the male bud or heart of the banana plant, and lotus flowers. I realize that ginger flowers have yet to appear in Southeast Asian markets on these shores, but I've included this wonderful recipe (adapted from Phia Sing's *Traditional Recipes of Laos*) for when the time comes. You can't go wrong substituting fresh ginger in this combination of chopped fresh shrimp, "three-layered" pork, lemon grass, shallots, and fish sauce.

½ *pound coarsely chopped fresh shrimp*

1 *pound fresh pork belly (uncured bacon), chopped*

½ *teaspoon freshly ground black pepper*

1 *ginger flower, washed with the flower petals separated, or 1 tablespoon minced fresh ginger*

3 *fresh chili peppers, minced*

2 *stalks lemon grass, minced*

4 *shallots, minced*

10 *sweet basil leaves, finely chopped*

2 *tablespoons fish sauce*

Salt to taste, ½ teaspoon or so

Pinch of sugar

1 *or 2 large banana leaves, cut into 10-inch by 6-inch sections, washed*

Wooden skewers or toothpicks

Mix together the chopped shrimp, pork, pepper, and ginger petals or minced fresh ginger. Mince the chilis, lemon grass, and shallots and pound in a mortar with the basil into a paste. Blend with the pork mixture and add the fish sauce, salt, and sugar.

Put a couple of tablespoons of the pork mixture on the banana leaf sections and fold and skewer to approximate the illustration. Cook over a medium charcoal fire for 6 to 7 mintues on each side. Stack the leaves on a platter and let guests help themselves. *Serves 6-8.*

Wrapped Banana Leaf

SOTO AJAM (Spicy Chicken Soup with Macadamia Nut Sambal) • Indonesia

I have a weakness for one-dish meals where eaters assemble their own food from a tableful of colorful ingredients. Here tamarind-flavored chicken shreds, clear noodles, fresh tomatoes, cucumbers, and coriander are put into individual bowls and covered by a fragrant broth. This is seasoned to taste with a fiery sambal of macadamia nuts, shrimp paste, and a squeeze of fresh lime.

1 4- to 5-pound chicken

10 cups water

¼ cup chopped onion

1 stalk lemon grass, finely sliced

3 cloves garlic, minced

1 teaspoon minced ginger

1½ teaspoons laos powder, or if fresh galangal is used, 3 ¼-inch slices

2 teaspoons coriander seeds, toasted in dry pan and ground

2 teaspoons cumin seeds, toasted in dry pan and ground

¾ teaspoon turmeric powder or 1 tablespoon finely minced fresh turmeric

1½ teaspoons freshly ground white pepper

1½ teaspoons sugar

Salt to taste, about 1½ teaspoons

1 walnut-sized piece tamarind pulp

⅓ cup warm water

Garnishes:

4 ounces Chinese vermicelli (peastarch or cellophane noodles)

1 cup fresh coriander leaves

2 medium yellow onions

½ cup peanut or vegetable oil

3 large ripe tomatoes, skinned, seeded, and cubed

2 cucumbers, peeled, halved, seeded, and sliced

2 or 3 limes, cut in half lengthwise and thinly sliced

Sambal:

Reserved oil from frying onions, above

12 macadamia nuts

½ ounce dried shrimp paste (¼-inch slice from an 8-ounce brick)

6 to 8 red chili peppers (use less if large)

1 1-inch cube fresh ginger

1 tablespoon light soy sauce

Cut the chicken into large pieces, cover with the water, and bring to a boil. Turn down the heat to medium and remove the scum and fat that come to the surface for the next 5 minutes. Turn the heat down further and add the onion, lemon grass, garlic, ginger, laos powder, ground coriander seeds, ground cumin, turmeric, white pepper, sugar, and salt to taste. Simmer for 30 minutes. Meanwhile, cover the tamarind with the warm water and allow to sit.

Put the vermicelli in a bowl and cover with boiling water. After 10 minutes, drain and cover the noodles with cold water. Slice the onions and fry them slowly in the peanut oil until brown and crisp. Drain on paper towels.

To make the sambal, strain the onion oil into a clean pan, or use fresh oil if you wish. Heat the oil and lightly brown the macadamia nuts. Remove the nuts with a slotted spoon and add the shrimp paste. Fry lightly on both sides in the hot oil. Turn off the heat. Remove the shrimp paste with a slotted spoon to a mortar, blender, or food processor. Cut the chili peppers into pieces with the seeds and add with the nuts, ginger, and soy sauce. Pound or blend the ingredients to a paste. Scrape into a serving dish and stir in 3 tablespoons of the oil that was used to fry the shrimp paste.

When the chicken is done, remove the pieces to a large platter. As soon as they are cool enough to handle, separate the meat from the bones, put the bones back into the simmering broth, and continue to cook. Slice the chicken meat or, better yet, shred it by hand. Strain the tamarind water through a sieve onto the chicken, forcing as much of it out as possible. Discard the pulp. Add a little salt to the chicken and toss. Heat a couple of tablespoons of the reserved onion cooking oil or fresh oil in a skillet or wok, and toss the chicken quickly over high heat for a minute or so. Remove to a serving dish. Decorate the rim of the dish with the lime slices. Put the crisp cooked onion on top of the chicken and put out on the table. Drain the vermicelli, put it in a serving dish and ring with coriander leaves. Place the tomatoes and cucumbers in a serving dish. Remove the bones from the broth and bring it to a boil, and either serve it in its pot or transfer it to a tureen. Put all on the table and instruct eaters as described in the recipe introduction. *Serves 6-8.*

Ginger in Japan and Korea

Japan

Ginger has been part of Japanese food and medicine for over a millenium. It was probably introduced from the Ch'in dynasty China in the third century B.C., when Japan was exposed to Chinese medicine.

Only the fresh rhizome of *Z. officinale* (*shōga*) is used in cooking. Its refreshing pungency is a distinctive characteristic of Japanese cuisine, which emphasizes sharp, clean tastes. The only other ginger used for food is an obscure relative, mioga (*Z. mioga*), and only its springtime shoots, not its rhizome, are eaten. All of the other Zingiberaceae, including dried ginger, turmeric, galangal, and cardamom, are important only as medicine.*

mioga Ginger Shoot with Grilled Fish

As in China, ginger is used with an eye to yin-yang harmony, and is especially valued with seafood, Japan's all-important source of protein. A striking difference between the Japanese use of ginger and its

---

* Japanese herbal medicine is far spicier than its cuisine. They traditionally don't use peppercorns; few others can say that. The seven-spice mixture, *shichimi*, contains two real spices, dried capsicum pepper flakes, and a spice unique to Japan, *sansho*, sometimes called Japanese pepper. Throw in the tear-producing mustard powder and the powder of Japan's own wasabi horseradish, and that's it.

use elsewhere in Asia is that it is never paired with garlic, which is simply not used in Japanese cooking in spite of Japan's being surrounded by the heaviest garlic consumption on earth. Ginger is rarely paired with anything that competes with its flavor and fragrance.

Pickles of ginger have assumed ritual importance in Japanese cuisine, and lend not only their pungency, but stunning visual effect to many Japanese dishes. Habitués of sushi bars are familiar with the pink *gari*, thin slices of pickled ginger, that are placed in front of them in a mound after they sit down. The red-dyed and pickled shoots of mioga ginger are served a stalk at a time as a garnish for grilled fish. Another brilliant red ginger pickle, the pungent *beni-shōga* presented in small rounds carefully placed, provides a striking taste and color counterpoint to shrimp and crabmeat.

Cooking with Ginger in Japan

Fresh ginger is most commonly grated in Japan. It even has its own tool, *oroshigane*, which it shares with *wasabi* horseradish, and has been used for centuries. The gratings are used in the array of dips that accompany dishes, or with rice vinegar and seasonings as dressing for the fastidiously composed cold plates known as *sunomono*, or *aemono*. The gratings are also squeezed through cheese cloth or by hand for ginger juice to season meat.[1] Ginger that is shredded into fine slivers to make stock called *shōga-ni*, or for use as a garnish, is less common.

Simmering. Water is the main cooking medium in Japanese cooking; simmering is the oldest technique. It is not a simple one. The processes for simmering foods are intricate and, according to seasonings and ingredients, vary to an extent that is bound to astonish most of us who merely toss ingredients in boiling water. Ginger broth is common for a variety of simmered ingredients, and shreds are a typical garnish. Ginger is standard as a de-fisher for mackerel and other oily fish.

Steaming. Steaming seafood with ginger works wonders, a fact upon which the Japanese and Chinese agree. Besides cooking fish and even abalone and other shellfish this way, the Japanese are fond of steamed chicken. To quote the eminent Shizuo Tsuji, "...the Japanese are definitely partial to chicken, which is steamed with a sprinkling of ginger juice and sake and eaten with a dipping sauce (which may include finely grated fresh ginger)."[2]

Sushi and Sashimi. Vinegared ginger (*gari*, or more formally, *sushōga*) is served with the vinegared rice rolls known as sushi in order to cleanse the palate between offerings and heighten the taste of freshness in the seafood. A grated ginger and soy sauce dip known as *shōga-joya* is served with sashimi—the latter being the deftly cut and arranged slices of raw fish.

Tempura. For traditional tempura, an assortment of vegetables and sometimes seafood fried in an airy batter, grated ginger is part of the traditional dipping sauce, along with grated daikon, soy sauce, mirin, and *dashi*, the basic Japanese stock (see Special Ingredients, page 43). I have included in the recipes that follow an intriguing tempura pancake (*kaki age*) which uses shredded ginger as an ingredient.

Korea

Korean cuisine seems to be a blend of delicate Japanese and hearty northern Chinese influences in both ingredients and techniques. There is a fine sashimi in Korea, as well as hot pots, soup-stews, and dishes flavored with bean sauce. Like their neighbors, the Koreans use only fresh ginger, and they share the Japanese fondness for the spring shoots of mioga ginger. Sometimes juice from ginger gratings is used, but more often the fresh rhizome is minced and a teaspoon or so is used to season most dishes. Marinades for grilled meats and poultry, common in Korea, typically include fresh ginger.

The tablespoon or so of freshly minced garlic that spikes most every dish is the most un-Japanese aspect in Korean cooking. The pickle *kimchi*, Korea's most famous dish, relies on a healthy dose of fresh ginger, twice as much garlic, a searing amount of ground dried red chilis, salt, and daikon juice. More than "pickled cabbage," its usual translation, *kimchi* is sustenance that graces the table every day and is particularly vital during Korea's bitter-cold winters. Authentic versions include Chinese celery cabbage and daikon, small fermented shrimp, raw seafood such as squid, and oysters. In elaborate versions, chestnuts, red dates, and Korea's highly esteemed pine nuts are included.

NOTES — JAPAN AND KOREA

1. As anyone who read *Shogun* knows, traditionally the Japanese did not eat beef, considered it rank, were repulsed by it, and detected a certain odor in those who ate it. They overcame these prejudices after the "opening" of Japan in the 1830s and began to eat it in the late 1800s. Today Japan's hand-massaged cattle produce the world's finest meat, kobe beef. A little ginger juice, to the Japanese taste, attacks any lingering unpleasantness.
2. *Japanese Cooking, A Simple Art*, Shizuo Tsuji, Kodansha International, Tokyo, New York, and San Francisco, 1980, page 207.

KAKI AGE *(Tempura Pancakes)* • *Japan*

Tempura batter can be enhanced by a little finely grated, or minced, fresh ginger, particularly for seafood. These pancakes, with shrimp and vegetable shreds, are light enough to float away in a small breeze. As with any tempura, they must be served immediately or they'll get soggy.

24 small shrimp (36-40 per pound), peeled, and cut in half lengthwise

⅓ cup finely shredded long white turnip (daikon or radish)

⅓ cup finely shredded carrot

2 tablespoons finely shredded ginger

½ cup peas, fresh or frozen

2 tablespoons or so roughly chopped coriander leaves

Batter:

½ cup flour (plus ¼ cup flour to be added later)

¾ cup water

1 teaspoon salt

1 egg yolk

1 teaspoon baking powder

½ teaspoon white pepper

Peanut or vegetable oil for deep-frying

Lemon slices for garnish

Put shrimp, turnip, carrot, ginger, peas, and coriander in a bowl. Mix the batter, add to the bowl, and stir well with a spoon.

Heat deep-frying oil to 375°F. Sift the remaining ¼ cup flour over the shrimp and vegetables and mix again. (The mixture should be thin.)

Scoop a couple of tablespoons of the mixture out of the bowl with a wide spatula, and gently slide it into the oil with a chopstick or knife.

Fry each pancake for a minute or so on each side until golden. Drain and serve with lemon slices. (Be sure to scoop out the inevitable fried batter crumbs between cooking the pancakes.) *Makes 16-18 pancakes.*

SALMON SIMMERED IN SAKE • *Japan*

Ginger is always used with dark-fleshed, oily fish, such as salmon, which poached gently with these seasonings brings out its best. This recipe also works well with East Coast bluefish or mackerel. You will need a pan with a bottom wide enough to hold the fish in one layer, and a slightly smaller lid, which will rest directly on the fish (the Japanese call this a drop-lid). This helps the seasonings penetrate, and keeps down the commotion of the bubbling hot liquid, which can damage the delicate fillets.

1½ to 2 pounds salmon fillet, with the skin; try to get a uniformly thick section

1 cup sake

¼ cup finely shredded ginger

1 teaspoon salt

1 teaspoon sugar

2 tablespoons light soy sauce

1 cup water or dashi

1½ cups grated daikon

½ teaspoon sesame oil

2 tablespoons scallion shreds

Crushed hot pepper flakes or Japanese seven-spice mixture

Rinse the fillet, remove any bones with tweezers, and cut into four pieces. Pour the sake into pan, sprinkle in ginger shreds, and lay the fish on top.

Bring to a boil over high heat, then reduce to a simmer. Place the lid gently on top of the fish and cook for 3 minutes.

After 3 minutes, pour the seasonings over the fish and allow to cook uncovered for another 2 to 3 minutes. Scatter the daikon over the fish, replace the lid, and cook for 1 minute. Turn off the heat, remove the lid, and gently remove the fillets to a warm serving platter, taking care that the ginger doesn't wash off.

Turn the heat to high and reduce the liquid remaining in the pan by half. Turn off the heat and sprinkle the sesame oil over the liquid, then spoon some of this sauce over the salmon, scatter the scallion shreds overall, and serve with the pepper flakes or seven-spices on the side. *Serves 4.*

GINGER STEAK WITH SHIITAKE MUSHROOMS • Japan

The juice squeezed from freshly grated ginger is a staple of Japanese cooking. Here it combines with sake to produce a mushroom sauce for pan-fried sirloin steak.

10 large dried shiitake mushrooms

1 tablespoon sesame oil

¼ cup mushroom soaking liquid

¼ cup sake or Chinese Shao hsing

1 tablespoon soy sauce

1 tablespoon ginger juice (grate a large knob of fresh ginger and squeeze it through cheesecloth)

1 teaspoon sugar (if you have it on hand substitute 1 tablespoon of mirin, the sweet Japanese cooking sake which is more characteristic)

2 pounds steak of your choice (two Delmonicos would do nicely)

1 teaspoon salt, or to taste

2 tablespoons peanut or vegetable oil

Soak the mushrooms in a bowl of hot water for 20 to 30 minutes. Remove when soft, squeeze the liquid out of them over the soaking bowl, cut them into thirds, toss with the sesame oil, and set aside.

Combine the ¼ cup of the mushroom soaking liquid, the sake, soy sauce, ginger juice, and sugar, and set aside. Sprinkle the salt lightly over both sides of the steaks.

Heat a skillet and add the oil. Sear the steaks; then cook them over medium heat for 3 minutes, or to taste. Turn them over and repeat. When done, remove them to a warm place.

Heat the skillet again and add the sake mixture, stirring to deglaze. After 2 minutes add the mushrooms and cook for a minute over high heat, then turn it off. Quickly slice the steak, arrange on a platter, pour the sauce over, and serve. *Serves 4.*

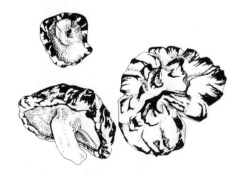

Dried Black mushrooms (Shiitake)

VINEGARED GINGER (Sushōga) • Japan

Also *gari* in sushi chefs' parlance, these paper-thin, pink-tinted slices are familiar to all sushi addicts. The pink tint comes naturally from the pickling. Do not wait to eat this until you have sushi. In Hong Kong, similarly pickled ginger is put on the table at finer restaurants as soon as you sit down, often as an accompaniment to the restaurant's own preserved (thousand year old) duck eggs.

1 pound fresh ginger (young is best)*
1 tablespoon salt
2 cups rice vinegar

1 cup water
6 tablespoons sugar

Clean the ginger with a damp paper towel; peel the skin if not using young ginger. Sprinkle with the salt and let sit overnight.

Mix the remaining ingredients and put in a jar with the ginger for at least a week. It will keep for months refrigerated. When serving the *sushoga*, slice paper-thin across the grain. *Makes 1 pound.*

---

* It's really best not to make this unless the pale-skinned, young ginger is available. If you can't get any, choose ginger that is as fiberless as possible. It will still have some bite.

SAENG PYEON (Ginger Candy with Pine Nuts) • Korea

Korean pinecones are the source of the tastiest species of pine nut found in Asian food markets and elsewhere. This wonderful native confection is rich but fresh tasting, and produces a warm afterglow.

1 cup peanut or corn oil

½ cup pine nuts

6 ounces ginger root

1 stick of cinnamon (1½-inch), or
  ½ teaspoon of powdered cinnamon

½ cup sugar

1 teaspoon salt

Heat the oil in a small wok or saucepan. When hot, turn off the heat and lightly brown the pine nuts, taking care not to burn. Remove to a paper towel. The oil should be saved for another purpose. When cool, chop the pine nuts coarsely and set aside.

Peel the ginger and simmer it in enough water to cover for 4 to 5 minutes, to take some of the bite out of it. When cool, dice finely. Set aside ⅔ cup.

Toast the cinnamon stick in a small dry skillet until fragrant, shaking the skillet so it won't burn. Crush to powder in a mortar and set aside ½ teaspoon.

Add the ginger, sugar, salt, and cinnamon to a heavy skillet or wok and cook, stirring, over medium heat until most of the moisture is gone and the mixture is sticky. Add the pine nuts and continue to stir until well mixed. Remove from heat.

When cool enough to handle, form the mixture into little balls or pull off odd-shaped pieces and allow to cool. *Makes about 1½ dozen candies.*

GINGER
EAST to WEST

FROM INDIA TO MOROCCO

India

India to the Middle East

Morocco

Ginger in India

Those who associate fresh ginger with East Asian cooking, as I did, may be surprised by the extent of its use in India. Not only is it added to most dishes (except, ironically, sweets and breads), but it is used in quantities that would elicit gasps from American cooks, even those who dabble in Eastern cookery. Meat dishes without a fistful of ginger are unusual. India is perhaps the only place that considers this moderately starchy rhizome a sauce thickener, demonstrating a fearless approach to its use.

India has always grown the biggest ginger crop, and some sources credit India with being the first to cultivate ginger, though there is no hard evidence. It may have been a native plant, but that, too, is conjecture. Ginger family members, however, thrive in the southern mountain jungles. Turmeric is most certainly native. It is used fresh, as ginger is used in the south, and is sacred to the Hindus.* The ginger plants that yield the familiar green cardamom pods, and the not-so-familiar black cardamom, and several varieties of galangal, grow wild in South India. Many of these gingers have medicinal uses, as they do elsewhere in Asia, but the Indians cook with an array of them, including obscure ones like mango ginger and zedoary.

Ginger was an early multipurpose tonic that has been around since the beginnings of medicine in India, just as it was in China. The Indians also considered good health to be a balance between heat and cold. Consequently, foods that could best maintain this balance, such as ginger, were the most highly prized. Ginger is still valued for its ability to stimulate the circulation and combat the innumerable cold-type ailments (see Ginger as Medicine, page 167). Ginger's reputation as a digestive aid, if not started in India, has been rigorously tested there. A major duty of the rhizome has been to calm stomachs under a relentless assault of peas, beans, and lentils. These legumes, called *dals*, are sustenance to India's millions of vegetarians, and are central to the diet of everyone.[1]

---

* A turmeric-soaked thread tied around the neck of the bride by her groom is the binding symbol of marriage.

Two Cuisines: North and South

In the markedly different cuisines of North and South India, food preparation always begins with ginger, while other spices and herbs are added in varying degrees. In the Moghul cooking of the north, with its familiar braised meats, kabobs, *kefta* (meat balls), and Tandoori-oven cooking, braising and grilling starts with a ginger-garlic-onion paste. In fact, two techniques that are a preliminary to braising meat and chicken, *geela masala tayyar karana* and *geela masala bhoonana*, are known to all northern cooks and concern the preparation of this paste and how to "slow-fry" it.

In the south the cooking is lighter, and overwhelmingly vegetarian; it is more likely to include coconut, tamarind, and tropical herbs like curry leaves, and fresh chilis. Here ginger is the most common ingredient in the spice pastes that are made up as a preliminary to most cooking. Hyderabadi cooks refer to a standard four ingredients—ginger, garlic, chilis, and turmeric. Among some vegetarian sects that do not eat noisome seasonings like garlic and onions, ginger acts alone.

Northern India cooks sometimes use dried ground ginger as well as fresh, even in the same dish. They are not interchangeable; each one serves a specific purpose. In fact, they are called by different names—the fresh is called *adrak*; the dried is called *sonth*. The Indian use of dried ginger got a boost in the sixteenth century from the Moghuls, whose cooking emulated the Persian cuisine. Ironically, the Persians used dried, rather than fresh spice, because their first ginger was shipped dried from India over the old caravan routes.

Cooking with Ginger in India

In Indian dishes the texture of the fresh ginger is not of the utmost concern. Usually chopped roughly, it is then ground with mortar and pestle (or blender) into a paste used for braising or grilling meats and poultry. Only in vegetable dishes and in some pickles and relishes is it shredded or minced for textural interest. Freshly minced ginger is occasionally sprinkled over rich *dals*.

Meat and Poultry

With few exceptions, meat is cooked with a lot of fresh ginger in India. It is a purifier and counteracts, or complements, the strong-flavored meats eaten in India: mutton, goat, and lamb. If the dish is to be braised, the common method we sometimes call a "curry," the slow frying of a ginger-onion-garlic combination to start the cooking process is standard. This paste is also the usual base for a marinade when meat is charcoal-grilled or roasted in the clay-lined tandoor. Fresh ginger is a seasoning for *keftas* (meat balls), and kabobs (skewered meat, ground or in chunks). The original Persian and Arabic versions use the dried spice.

The Indians were the first to cook an indigenous jungle fowl known today as the chicken. While it is an inexpensive source of protein welcomed around the world, in India its enjoyment is limited to persons of some means. In the south, there are sects who distinguish its consumption from that of red meat. Occasionally *chats*, cold appetizer-salads redolent of cumin, coriander, and chilis, include chicken, but never red meat. In the north, chicken is prepared in the same manner as other meats.

Seafood

In America most Indian restaurants and food experts are of the Moghul tradition. There is the misconception that Indians infrequently eat fish. Although not much seafood was available in the Moghul regions, there are some 3,000 miles of Indian coastline, not to mention a river or two. Consequently, Indians have been cooking wonderful fish and shellfish dishes for thousands of years, using fresh ginger, of course. The Indians use ginger in paste or minced form in most seafood dishes, but do not deem it a necessity as the Chinese do. The few northern fish dishes are heavy handed with spices and sauce, whereas the southern dishes excel with fragrant combinations of fresh ginger, coriander (seeds and fresh leaves), cumin seeds, a little garlic, chilis, coconut milk, and the ubiquitous turmeric, sometimes fresh sliced, a style of fish cookery akin to that of Southeast Asia.

Vegetables

Vegetables may be main courses or side dishes. They are cooked far longer than crisply colorful Chinese vegetables or even those of the West. This gives the spices a chance to permeate the dish. Ginger, though not added as routinely to vegetables as it is to meat, is nonetheless a prime accompaniment, and lends an important fresh taste. Fresh coriander also helps. In the Indian view, the natural flavors of the vegetable are awakened by the correct application of seasonings regardless of cooking time.[2] Ginger may be ground to a paste and fried before vegetables are added, or it may be used shredded or minced.

Dals (Legumes)

This ancient category of Indian foods is the society's most important protein source, especially for the tens of millions who eat no meat. In Indian cooking, dals are as distinct from vegetables as meats or poultry. They are incorporated into everything, from deep-frying batters to bread and desserts. As part of a meal, a dal may be a hearty main course or a soup-like puree served in a small cup. Ginger is routine, not only for digestion, but as a refreshing and light counterpoint to their warming richness.

Relishes, Chutneys, and Pickles

Both fresh and dried ginger are essential to many of the myriad appetite-stimulating relishes and chutneys served with Indian meals. They range from improvised, chopped raw vegetables, which are seasoned and allowed to stand no more than 30 minutes before serving, to elaborate chutneys of pureed fruit with nuts and spices, reserved for special meals.

Yoghurt accompaniments (*raitas*) are a subgroup which range from simple combinations of fine yoghurt and chopped fresh herbs to full-fledged salad-type side dishes with cooked ingredients. Chopped fresh ginger, fresh coriander, fresh chilis, and mint combined with yoghurt are a perfect complement to grilled or braised meats. In the south these *raitas* or *pachadis* (with mustard seeds) substitute coconut milk or fine shreds of coconut for the less available dairy product. Ginger, always fresh in this region, is a mainstay.

Indians have been pickling everything edible, from mangoes to partridges, as long as their cuisine has existed.[3] Ginger plays a major role as both seasoning and ingredient, where the simplest pickle can be nothing more than the chopped, fresh rhizome and boiled lime juice.

Sweets

For a country where ginger and sugarcane may be native,[4] astonishingly, the two are rarely combined. Ginger is simply not used in India's endless variety of puddings, sweetmeats, and confections, nor are most spices, except cardamom, once in a while saffron, and occasionally a pinch of nutmeg or cloves.

NOTES — INDIA

1. Ginger has help in India from asafetida, a combination of smelly gum resins, which is possibly the only seasoning used primarily for digestion.
2. The properly spiced dish, as a Hyderabadi saying goes, should "taste awake but not angry."
3. We get our pickling techniques from the English, who got theirs directly from India. Even the dill pickle is probably of Indian origin since dill is a staple and may have been native; cucumber cultivation in India goes back at least 3,000 years.
4. Sugarcane is thought to be native to the Bay of Bengal, where it spread throughout South Asia, and was a staple crop before the sweet-crazy West had an inkling of its existence.

LAMB KORMA WITH ALMONDS (Gosht Korma Badaami) • India

The toasting of spices is a standard preliminary to braised meat dishes in Moghul cooking. The dish below, with lamb, butter, and cream, is quite rich, and is also refined and elegant since there is a direct correlation between animal fat and fine food in the Moghul cuisine.

¼ cup blanched almonds, preferably the small Asian variety

2 teaspoons cumin seeds

4 dried chili peppers

1 1-inch cinnamon stick

½ cup clarified butter or peanut oil

3 pounds boneless shoulder or leg of lamb, cut into 1½-inch cubes

1½ cups sliced onions

3 tablespoons chopped fresh ginger

1½ tablespoons finely chopped garlic

1 teaspoon mace

½ teaspoon ground nutmeg

1 teaspoon sweet paprika

1 cup sour cream

1 cup heavy cream

1 cup milk

1 tablespoon salt, or to taste

½ teaspoon white pepper

1 teaspoon garam masala

Fresh coriander leaves for garnish

Place the almonds, cumin, chili peppers, and cinnamon stick in a dry skillet and toast over medium heat, shaking the pan until fragrant. (The almonds should begin to brown.) Remove the spices to a grinder, or mortar, and pulverize. Set aside.

Heat half the butter in a heavy skillet or wok and brown the lamb in two batches, leaving the butter in the pan each time you remove the lamb. (This is best done with a slotted spoon.) Add the remaining ¼ cup butter to the pan, and over medium-high heat, cook the onions, stirring continuously, about 10 minutes or until they are caramel brown. Add the ginger and garlic and fry another 2 minutes. Stir in the mace, nutmeg, and paprika. Then add the lamb and toss to coat. Sprinkle on the almond mixture and continue to mix.

Add the sour cream, ½ cup of the heavy cream, and the milk. Bring to a boil, add the salt, and turn the heat to low. Cover and simmer for 2 hours, stirring frequently to prevent sticking. (Add a little milk if it becomes too dry.) The meat should be done after 2 hours and there should be little sauce left. Sprinkle the pepper and *garam masala* into the sauce, pour over the remaining cream, and stir just to heat. Serve garnished with fresh coriander. *Serves 4-6.*

ADRAK (Fresh Ginger) SOUP • India

It's difficult to choose a category for this. It's an effective cold remedy; but it is also an unusual light broth that works well as a prelude, or better still, a follow-up to a rich North African, Middle Eastern, or Indian meal. It is, at the least, comment-provoking to serve it hot from a mug on a chilly day—more strangely, hot from a mug on a hot day, which, as the Indians know, will cool you off.

2 rounded tablespoons grated fresh
  ginger with the juice
4 cups water or chicken broth
¾ teaspoon salt, or to taste
1 tablespoon cumin seeds toasted in a
  dry skillet and ground

½ teaspoon freshly ground pepper
Juice of one lemon
Fresh coriander leaves for garnish

Bring the grated ginger and water, or broth, to a boil, then simmer about 30 minutes. The liquid will have reduced to half. Add the salt, cumin, and pepper and simmer for 2 minutes longer. Squeeze in the lemon juice, garnish with the coriander leaves, and serve. *Serves 4-6.*

CHICKEN IN APRICOT-CORIANDER SAUCE • India

Combinations of meat or poultry with fruit are distinctly Moghul, of Persian influence. This simple braised dish uses both fresh and dried ginger in a tangy, lightly spiced sauce that is like a delicate chutney.

1 3½- to 4-pound chicken
Salt
1 teaspoon ground ginger
1¼ cups unsulfured dried apricots
2 cups loosely packed coriander leaves
  and stems
½ cup clarified butter or peanut oil, or
  more if necessary
1 cup chopped onion
3 tablespoons finely minced ginger

1 3-inch cinnamon stick
8 green cardamom pods (or 1 teaspoon
  ground)
¼ teaspoon ground cloves
1 teaspoon freshly ground white pepper
1½ cups fresh peeled and chopped ripe
  plum tomatoes (or canned Italian
  plum tomatoes)
Fresh coriander leaves for garnish

Skin the chicken* and cut into serving pieces. Rub 1 teaspoon salt and the ground ginger over the chicken pieces and let stand for an hour. Meanwhile, put the apricots in a bowl, cover with 1½ cups boiling water, and let soak for 45 minutes. Remove the apricots, reserving the soaking liquid, to a food processor or blender, add the coriander, reserving a few leaves for garnish, and blend until smooth.

Heat half the butter or oil in a heavy skillet or wok. Brown the chicken a few pieces at a time, removing them with a slotted spoon to a bowl. When the chicken is browned, add the rest of the butter and fry the onion, stirring constantly until it is light brown. Add the fresh ginger, cinnamon stick, and cardamom pods and cook, stirring, for another 2 minutes. Add the cloves and the white pepper, and stir briefly to blend. Add the reserved apricot soaking liquid, the tomatoes, 1 teaspoon salt, and the apricot puree and bring to a boil. Add the chicken pieces, and bring to a boil again. Cover, turn the heat to low, and let simmer for 45 minutes, stirring from time to time. You may have to add more liquid or adjust the heat.

When the chicken is done, remove it to a warm serving platter. If the sauce is thin, reduce it to a desired consistency. Check the seasoning and pour the sauce over the chicken. Garnish with coriander leaves and serve. *Serves 4.*

* When I first came across instructions in Indian cookbooks to remove the skin of a chicken, I thought it was in deference to an American readership that balks at excess fat. Certainly this wouldn't bother Indian eaters. In the words of Julie Sahni, however, "In Indian cooking, the chicken is always—I mean always—skinned before being cooked . . . Indians believe the skin to be unclean and, along with feathers, beak, and other inedible parts, not to be eaten." *Classic Indian Cooking*, p. 205.

NEW POTATOES WITH PEAS AND CORIANDER • India

This vegetable dish is just as tasty served cold or at room temperature—like a spicy potato salad—as it is hot.

6 to 8 small new potatoes

¼ cup peanut or vegetable oil

1 teaspoon cumin seeds

½ teaspoon turmeric powder (or 2 teaspoons fresh)

1½ tablespoons minced fresh ginger

2 small red chili peppers, coarsely chopped

1 cup chopped fresh coriander

1¼ teaspoons salt, or to taste

1 teaspoon garam masala

1 tablespoon ground coriander seeds

¼ cup lemon juice

6 tablespoons water

½ cup fresh or frozen peas

Wash and dice the potatoes with the skin. Put them in water to cover until ready to use.

Heat the oil in a skillet. Drain the potatoes and add to the skillet with the cumin seeds. Cook, stirring, for 2 minutes; then add the turmeric, ginger, and peppers. Cook, stirring, another 3 minutes.

Add the rest of the ingredients except the peas, lower the heat, cover, and simmer for 15 minutes, checking from time to time to make sure there's still liquid. Add a little water, if necessary.

Add the peas just before serving. Remove the cover, turn up the heat, and cook, stirring, until most of the liquid is gone. *Serves 4-6.*

ROASTED EGGPLANT WITH CHILIS • India

This dish is as useful as it is tasty. It is simply made and, as with most eggplant dishes, can be prepared ahead of time and served at room temperature.

2 pounds eggplant (Western or Oriental)

½ cup olive or peanut oil

2 cups finely chopped onion

1 cup ripe tomatoes (or canned Italian plum tomatoes), peeled, seeded, and cut into wedges

½ cup finely shredded fresh ginger

1½ teaspoons salt, or to taste

½ cup or more fresh red or green chili peppers, shredded

1 tablespoon sweet paprika

½ teaspoon freshly ground black pepper

½ cup chopped parsley or fresh coriander

Grill the whole eggplants over hot charcoals, turning from time to time, until they collapse.* If no grill is available, you may broil them. Let sit until cool enough to handle, then cut them open and scrape the pulp into a skillet with the oil. Add the onion and cook over medium heat for 10 minutes, stirring frequently to prevent scorching.

Add the tomatoes, ginger, salt, peppers, paprika, and black pepper. Cook, stirring often, for 10 to 15 minutes. Be careful that it does not burn. When done, stir in the parsley or coriander and turn off the heat. *Serves 4-6.*

* Oriental eggplants will cook in half the time it takes Western eggplants to cook.

DRY-FRIED STRING BEANS WITH INDIAN SPICES

This hybrid combines a Chinese method of cooking string beans, dry-frying (which used to mean beans wrinkled under glass in the hot sun, but now refers to deep-frying them), and Indian seasonings. It's equally good hot, cold, or at room temperature.

1½ pounds green beans or Chinese long beans, cut into 3-inch sections

2 cups peanut oil

2 to 4 fresh chili peppers, shredded

2 tablespoons shredded ginger

1 teaspoon ground coriander

1 teaspoon garam masala

¼ teaspoon turmeric

4 tablespoons lemon juice

2 tablespoons dry sherry

1 teaspoon salt, or to taste

½ teaspoon sugar

1 teaspoon cumin seeds

¼ cup chopped fresh coriander

Remove tough ends of beans and discard. Heat oil in a wok or skillet until nearly smoking, and fry the beans until wrinkled, about 5 minutes. Remove them and drain. Put the chili shreds and ginger together and set aside. Mix the ground coriander, *garam masala*, and turmeric and set aside. Then mix the lemon juice, sherry, salt, and sugar and set aside.

Drain the oil from the pan, leaving 2 tablespoons. Over high heat cook the cumin seeds, briefly, then add the combined spices. Stir 10 seconds and add the ginger and chili peppers. Continue to stir for 20 seconds. Toss in the beans and stir rapidly to coat with the spices. Pour in the lemon juice/sherry mixture. Stir this over high heat until most of the juice is gone, then stir in the coriander leaves and serve. *Serves 4-6.*

PALAK DAL—Spinach and Lentil Stew • India

This unusually attractive dal is fun to eat, with people creating their own dishes from the available condiments. The base is a hearty stew of lentils into which fresh spinach is swirled at the last minute, adding its brilliant green. Next, onions that have been slowly browned in oil are added. Each person tops a bowlful with sour cream, *hara masala* (a fragrant blend of herbs and fresh chili), and minced fresh ginger.

Be forewarned: a little of this warming nourishment goes a long way, which is why ginger is standard to dals as a digestive aid as well as a seasoning. A delicious supper can be made of a couple of helpings, some salad, and Indian bread.

1½ cups lentils
5 cups water
2 large onions
6 cloves garlic
2 teaspoons salt, or to taste
½ teaspoon ground ginger
6 tablespoons peanut or vegetable oil

½ pound chopped fresh spinach
1 cup sour cream
¼ cup finely minced fresh ginger
Hara Masala:
½ cup fresh coriander leaves and stems
¼ cup fresh mint leaves
¼ cup small green chili peppers

If the lentils are not the packaged variety, pick them over carefully and rinse well. Put the lentils in a heat-proof casserole and cover with water. Chop one of the onions, mince 2 garlic cloves, and add to the pot with the salt and ground ginger. Bring to a boil, reduce the heat, and simmer until the lentils begin to fall apart, about 45 minutes.

Meanwhile, prepare the *hara masala*: Chop and combine the coriander, mint, and chili peppers and set aside.

Slice the remaining onion and garlic lengthwise. About 20 minutes before the lentils are done, heat the oil in a heavy skillet. Add the onions and garlic and cook them slowly over gentle heat, stirring frequently to prevent scorching. When the onions are a deep golden brown, remove the pan from the heat.

When the lentils are tender, transfer the stew to a tureen (or leave it in the pot if it will be served that way). Stir in the spinach and pour the browned onions over the top. Put the sour cream, fresh ginger, and *hara masala* in separate bowls on the table for people to help themselves. *Serves 6-8.*

INDIAN VICHYSSOISE • South India

Originally a rich *pachadi*, the south Indian counterpart of *raita*, this thinner version makes an unusually delicious cold potato soup.

4 *large potatoes*

1 *large onion, finely chopped*

4 *fresh green chilis, finely chopped*

¼ *cup butter*

1 *tablespoon finely minced ginger*

1½ *cups thick, unsweetened coconut milk*

3 *cups chicken stock*

2 *teaspoons salt, or to taste*

¾ *cup plain yoghurt*

2 *hot dried chilis*

1 *tablespoon mustard seeds*

Sprigs of mint for garnish

Peel and dice the potatoes, and drop them into cold water as you go. Rinse, then simmer them in a large quantity of water until they can be easily pierced with a fork. Drain and roughly mash.

In a large pot, cook the onion and chilis in butter until the onion is transparent. Add the potatoes, ginger, and coconut milk. Beat this mixture until thick and smooth. Add the stock and salt, and bring to a boil while stirring. Turn off the heat. Stir in the yoghurt and refrigerate.

Toast the dried chilis and mustard seeds in a dry skillet until the mustard seeds begin to pop. Grind this mixture into a coarse powder. Serve the chilled soup with the mint sprigs and spices on the side. *Serves 6-8.*

Two Indian Accompaniments

Fresh Carrot Relish is the sort of improvised chutney that is rapidly made by the home cook from ingredients on hand to complement whatever dishes have been simmering on the stove. It clears the palate between bites of the main course. It could be as modest as chopped ginger or chopped onions with a shot of lime juice.

Raita is another improvised accompaniment that is delicious with the braised lamb dishes in this section.

FRESH CARROT RELISH

½ pound carrots, finely chopped

1 small onion, finely chopped

3 tablespoons finely chopped fresh coriander leaves

1½ tablespoons finely chopped fresh ginger

Juice of 1 lime

1 green chili, finely chopped with seeds

1 teaspoon salt

¼ teaspoon freshly ground black pepper

Mix together all ingredients and let marinate 30 minutes before serving. *Makes 1 cup.*

RAITA

1 cup yoghurt

½ cup sour cream

2 tablespoons finely minced fresh ginger

2 tablespoons finely minced fresh coriander leaves

1 tablespoon finely minced green chili, with seeds

1 tablespoon finely minced mint leaves

1 tablespoon freshly squeezed lemon juice

Combine all the ingredients. Let sit for 30 minutes and serve. *Serves 4-8.*

SOUR EGGPLANT PICKLES · *Iran*

Pickling eggplant is common from the Middle East to Southeast Asia. In Thailand, tiny pea eggplants are used only for pickling. Those below are more of a condiment to go with Middle Eastern or Indian food. The tamarind-vinegar combination produces a mouth-puckering sourness that heightens the taste of whatever they are served with. Children probably won't get into them.

2 pounds small Asian eggplant	*2 teaspoons fennel seeds*
1 cup or more cider vinegar	*6 cloves garlic*
1 tablespoon sugar	*2 tablespoons chopped fresh ginger*
Piece of tamarind the size of a walnut	*1 teaspoon or more cayenne*
1 tablespoon white mustard seeds	*2 teaspoons black pepper*
1 tablespoon coriander seeds	*2 teaspoons salt*

Preheat the oven to 350°F. Pierce the eggplants all over with a fork and bake on the oven rack 30 minutes until soft. (Put a pan underneath to catch any juices.) When they're cool enough to handle, peel the eggplants and cut the flesh into ½-inch cubes. Mix with ½ cup of the vinegar and the sugar.

Soak the tamarind in hot water for 15 minutes. Rub it and break it apart with your fingers; then press it with the liquid through a sieve into the eggplant.

Toast all the seeds in a warm skillet until fragrant, then blend with the garlic, ginger, and ¼ cup of the vinegar to a paste, either in a mortar or a blender. Add this paste to the eggplants with the remaining ¼ cup of vinegar (more vinegar may be required to cover the eggplant), cayenne, pepper, and salt. *Makes about 1 quart.*

Note: This will keep indefinitely if transferred to a sterilized jar and refrigerated.

India to the Middle East

While the use of fresh ginger spread throughout eastern Asia, the dried spice became a fixture of the cuisines west of India. The cooking we call Middle Eastern, with Persian and Arabic roots, still uses only dried ginger. This is a matter of preference; originally there was no choice.

The caravan trails heading west out of India are approximately 5,000 years old. When ginger became a popular trading commodity is not known, but these routes over mountains and through deserts were not conducive to transporting anything fresh, nor would the weight of fresh ginger have been welcome. The climate in the regions along the way was not suited to ginger cultivation. Over the centuries Persian and Arab cuisines refined their use of ginger as a spice, along with many other fragrant roots, barks, and berries from the East. Even today, with the fresh rhizome available, the cuisines call for it dried and ground.

The Persians were the first to adopt ginger; although when this happened, or when ginger finally reached the Mediterranean, cannot be determined exactly. Its use in the Middle East predates the cooking of the Greeks and Romans, for whom ginger was a well-documented passion. Etymological sleuthing has turned up words for ginger in Assyrian and Babylonian, antecedents of Latin by 1,000 years or so.[1]

Ginger was used in ancient Egypt,[2] undoubtedly taken there by the Mediterranean's earliest dealers, the Phoenicians. With the ascension of Islam in the seventh century, the spicy Middle Eastern cuisine we know spread as far east as India and westward through North Africa to Spain.

NOTES — INDIA TO THE MIDDLE EAST

1. My colleague and Middle Eastern language expert Charles Perry did the etymological sleuthing. He also points out that turmeric may have preceded ginger in the West, since the word for it apparently did. Ginger in Assyrian translates as "turmeric of the mountain."

2. I have seen in food writings that the Egyptians used ginger in the sixth century B.C. The hieroglyph that supposedly signalled this use has turned out to be "wild ginger," a plant of no relation. The Phoenicians probably showed up with Z. *officinale* a couple thousand years later.

107

GINGER

Ginger in Morocco

E ach Middle Eastern and North African cuisine holds its own
fascination, but I decided to select only one of these dried ginger
cuisines. The natural ingredients and indigenous peoples of each land
are unique, yet their use of ground ginger does not differ enough to
examine in this book. These cuisines share a common appreciation of
the subtle differences in ginger's quality as a spice. The markets
throughout the Middle East sell it in varying grades.

I chose Morocco, not because it best represents Middle Eastern
cooking, but because ginger in this Mediterranean region, far from
Asia, is combined with an important array of foods—olives, almonds,
dried fruit, herbs such as sage, thyme, and bay, even hashish in a
candy called *majoun*. Ginger reached Morocco long ago, perhaps via the
Phoenicians. The native Berbers adapted their traditional cooking,
such as whole roasts of sheep and couscous, to these Eastern spices.
Much later, in the seventh century, an invasion by Moslem Arabs
brought new uses for ginger.

Mostly, I was sold on the food of Morocco before even taking a bite,
by the aroma of a chicken tajine (stew is an unjust description) flavored with a yellow sauce of ginger and saffron, and topped by what is
now a staple in my kitchen, preserved lemons.

Cooking with Ginger in Morocco

Ginger (*skinjbir*) in Morocco is sold by grade, according to origin and
curing method. The top grade is bleached pure white (*skinjbir bied*), also
known as limed ginger, and is favored throughout the Middle East.
India is its usual source. Among other ginger family members, turmeric is a primary spice, and the green and black cardamom pods are
also important. Other Zingiberaceae are found in the world's most
intriguing spice blend—*ras-el-hanout*—specifically galangal, and grains
of paradise, which are indigenous to Africa.

The Tajine
A teaspoon more or less of freshly ground ginger is basic to this
fragrant casserole, which in turn is basic to Moroccan cooking. To put

the necessary distance between tajine and a mundane stew, one should conjure up all that is savory, succulent, and delicately perfumed. A tajine is traditionally cooked in a clay vessel over fire, sometimes at the bottom of a *couscousïere*, where its vapors steam the semolina grains called couscous.

Tajine combinations are as broad as the Moroccan cuisine, but usually involve meat or poultry, by themselves or with vegetables and legumes. Ginger combines with saffron (sometimes supplemented by a pinch of turmeric) in the basic tajine yellow sauce, *m'qualli*, pronounced "makalli." The fat used in this sauce is usually either olive oil or peanut oil, sometimes butter; and standard additions are the uniquely delicious Moroccan preserved lemons (see page 47) and olives. A tajine red sauce common with meats, *m'chermel*, pronounced "emshmel," is simply the yellow sauce with the addition of cumin and a healthy dose of sweet paprika.

Other common tajines combine fruit, such as quince, apples, pears, prunes, and dates, with meat and occasionally chicken. Ginger, cinnamon, and black pepper provide pungency, and thick honey is sometimes added.

Tajines with *keftas* are a unique North African use of these Middle Eastern meatballs which are also grilled in Morocco as elsewhere. Hand-chopped lamb is seasoned with ginger, other spices and fresh herbs, and the mixture is kneaded and allowed to rest, as bread is, for smooth texture and added flavor.

Chermoula

This is a hot-flavored marinade or sauce of olive oil that is flavored with ginger, garlic, cumin, vinegar, or lemon juice, and other herbs and spices. The composition varies by region. It is especially pleasing with fish, and might well be adapted, as I have done in the recipe section, to grilled foods.

Salads

In Morocco, salads encompass a variety of cold plates that stimulate the appetite before the first tajine. They may be cooked or raw, and the combinations, from oranges with olives, to beets with paprika, to lambs' brains with preserved lemons, are exotic and colorful. Ginger is not *de rigueur*, but is used often.

Ras-el-Hanout

This all-purpose spice blend and aphrodisiac mixture employs upwards of thirteen spices, sometimes more than fifty. Even the simplest contain a variety of ginger family members—always a couple of grades of ground ginger, turmeric, and at least one cardamom. Galangal and grains of paradise are also fairly standard. And lest these don't cause a warm glow, *ras-el-hanout* is laced with belladonna berries, and traces of the beetle, *Lytta vesicatoria*, known as Spanish fly. Tamer combinations are available at Middle Eastern spice shops in the United States.

B'steeya

This world-renowned pigeon pie is wrapped in a kind of filo called *warka*. It is always seasoned with the finest ground ginger in combination with cinnamon, saffron, almonds, and lemon.

I have not included any methods for preparing couscous or b'steeya among the recipes that follow, although ginger flavors these dishes and they are the most esteemed in the Moroccan cuisine. Given the scope of this book, I felt it already enough to require the reader to make preserved lemons for the dish or two that need them. For those who want to pursue Moroccan cuisine, I recommend highly Paula Wolfert's uncompromising *Couscous and Other Good Food from Morocco* or the works of Lafita Bennani Smires.

GRILLED FISH WITH MARINADE · Morocco

This fish, cooked over charcoal, will be devoured unmercifully. The marinade, *chermoula*, with its flavor of garlic, lemon, and cumin, goes well with any mild-flavored fish. Using fresh ginger rather than ground (as is usually done in Moroccan cooking), along with a chopped fresh chili, adds a little heat.

1 mild-flavored, white-fleshed fish, 2 to 3 pounds, cleaned, with the head on

¼ cup or more pitted and chopped green olives (use a good Middle Eastern or Italian variety)

1 lemon, thinly sliced

2 tablespoons lightly chopped mint leaves

Marinade:

2 teaspoons cumin seeds

1 bunch fresh coriander

1 fresh hot chili pepper

4 cloves garlic

1 1-inch cube fresh ginger

¼ cup fresh lemon juice

¼ cup water

1 tablespoon paprika

2 teaspoons salt

½ teaspoon sugar or honey

½ cup olive or peanut oil

Toast the cumin seeds in a dry skillet until fragrant. Add the cumin to a food processor or blender with all the remaining marinade ingredients except the oil. Blend to a fine paste. Remove the paste to a bowl and gently stir in the oil.

Score the fish lightly with diagonal cuts 1 inch apart. In a large bowl, pour the marinade over the fish, spreading it with the fingers to make sure the fish is coated entirely. Let stand at least 1 hour while you prepare a charcoal fire of medium heat.*

When the fire is ready, oil the grill liberally to keep the fish from sticking. Grill the fish 8 to 10 minutes on each side, basting it with ¼ cup of the marinade. The fish is done when a skewer easily penetrates the thickest part of the flesh.

After turning the fish, heat the remaining marinade to near boiling and add the olives and lemon slices. Keep warm until the fish is ready to serve. Then transfer the fish to a serving platter, pour the hot marinade over, and garnish with mint leaves. *Serves 4.*

---

* The fish may be broiled on aluminum foil, in which case the entire marinade should be poured over at the start, including the olives and lemon slices. Save the mint leaves until the end.

CHICKEN WITH PRUNES, HONEY, AND ALMONDS • Morocco

The sauce of this chicken and fruit tajine is luxurious, saffron-scented, and sweetened with honey. The whole dish gleams, and is rendered even more inviting by a sprinkling of toasted sesame seeds.

1 heaping cup unsulfured prunes

3- to 4-pound chicken with giblets (optional)

¼ cup sweet butter

2 chopped onions

1½ teaspoons ground ginger, or 2 tablespoons minced fresh ginger

1 cup water

1 2-inch cinnamon stick

Healthy pinch of saffron threads soaked in ¼ cup hot water

1½ teaspoons salt, or to taste

½ teaspoon freshly ground black pepper

2 tablespoons sesame seeds

4 ounces blanched whole almonds, preferably the small Asian variety

4 tablespoons thick honey, slightly more if regular honey is used

4 small red chili peppers, quartered lengthwise

Pit the prunes and soak in 2 cups of warm water for 30 minutes. Drain and set aside, reserving 1 cup of the soaking liquid.

Cut the chicken into 8 to 10 pieces with the bone, or have your butcher do it. Trim and score the gizzard and set it aside with the liver and heart, if you are choosing to use the giblets.

Heat the butter in a large, heavy skillet and add the chicken, giblets, onions, and ginger, and cook stirring over medium-high heat for 4 minutes. Add the water, reserved prune liquid, cinnamon stick, saffron with soaking liquid, salt, and pepper. Bring to a boil, lower the heat, cover and simmer for 45 minutes.

Meanwhile toast the sesame seeds in a dry skillet until fragrant, shaking the pan to keep them from burning. Remove and set aside. Toast the almonds on a baking sheet in the oven and set aside.

With a slotted spoon, remove the chicken to a warm serving platter or casserole, leaving the sauce in the pan. Cover the chicken to keep it warm. Add the honey, red peppers, and prunes to the sauce. Turn the heat to medium and cook the sauce for 8 minutes. Remove the prunes and peppers to the chicken platter with a slotted spoon.* Turn the heat to high and reduce the sauce to a thin syrup.

Arrange the chicken, prunes, almonds, and peppers on the platter and pour the sauce over them. Sprinkle with the sesame seeds and serve. *Serves 4.*

* The chicken may be returned to the sauce briefly to reheat just before you are about to remove the prunes and peppers.

CHICKEN WITH OLIVES AND PRESERVED LEMONS • Morocco

Try this dish adapted from Paula Wolfert's fine Moroccan cookbook and you'll take up the cuisine. Its flavors and texture hint at the great pigeon pie, *b'steeya*. In fact, squabs may be substituted for the chicken, since this preparation is standard with either. This recipe is not difficult, and best demonstrates the extraordinary combination of ginger and saffron.

1 chicken, 3½ pounds, cut into 8 to 10 pieces (or 3 1-pound squabs)*

Salt

½ cup finely chopped onion

1 tablespoon finely minced garlic

1 teaspoon ground ginger, or 1 tablespoon finely minced fresh

½ cup chopped coriander leaves

Pinch of saffron threads soaked in 2 tablespoons hot water

1 2-inch cinnamon stick

½ teaspoon freshly ground black pepper

5 tablespoons olive oil

1½ cups water

6 eggs

¼ cup chopped parsley

Peel of two preserved lemons, diced (see page 47)

6 fine Greek or Italian green or tan olives, pitted and coarsely chopped

¼ cup fresh lemon juice

Preheat oven to 350°F. Rub the chicken pieces with 1 teaspoon of salt and let stand 1 hour. Rinse, dry, and arrange in a casserole. Add the onion, garlic, ginger, coriander leaves, saffron and soaking water, cinnamon, pepper, olive oil, and water, and bring to a boil.

Cover and simmer for 50 minutes or until the meat starts to fall off the bone. Take the chicken out of the casserole, and reduce the sauce until it thickens. There should be about 1½ cups. Return the chicken pieces to the sauce.

Beat the eggs until just blended, and add the parsley, lemon peel, and olives. Pour this mixture into the casserole, cover, and bake for 20 minutes. Remove the cover, turn the oven up to 550°F, and cook until the chicken and egg are lightly browned, 10 to 15 minutes. Sprinkle with the lemon juice and serve. *Serves 4.*

* If squabs are used, quarter each, and treat as you do the chicken. While the squabs are more flavorful, they're also bonier. In either case the meat comes off easily.

MOROCCAN GRILLED CHICKEN LEGS

This unorthodox method of barbecuing is adapted from a Moroccan method for grilling pigeons. (To substitute them for chicken, remove the backbones and flatten the whole birds, and simmer them a couple of minutes longer than the chicken.) The initial simmering ensures that the seasonings permeate the meat, cuts down on the grilling time, and produces a more tender result.

1 1-inch cube fresh ginger
6 garlic cloves
1 fresh chili pepper
1 onion
1 bunch parsley
1 bunch fresh coriander
½ cup fresh lemon juice
¼ cup olive oil

1 tablespoon cumin seeds
1 tablespoon paprika
3 cups water
2 teaspoons salt
½ teaspoon sugar
5 pounds whole chicken legs (leg and thigh)
Lemon slices for garnish

In a food processor or blender finely chop the ginger, garlic, chili pepper, onion, parsley, and coriander with the lemon juice.

In a pot big enough to hold the chicken legs with room to spare, heat the oil and add the cumin seeds. Cook until fragrant, then add the contents of the food processor and the paprika. Cook, stirring, for 1 minute. Add the water, salt, and sugar and bring to a boil.

Add the chicken legs to the pot. When the water comes to a boil again, turn down the heat, cover, and simmer for 10 minutes. Remove the legs from the sauce and set them aside to cool. (You may refrigerate the legs at this point.)

Turn the heat under the sauce to high and reduce to about a cup. (It should be bubbly and oily.) Remove from the heat. When cool, pour the sauce over the chicken legs and mix thoroughly. Marinate the legs for at least 3 hours, or overnight in the refrigerator.

Remove the chicken from the refrigerator at least an hour before cooking. Grill the legs over a hot charcoal fire for 6 to 8 minutes on a side, basting from time to time with a little of the marinade. When they are done, arrange them on a serving platter, heat the remaining sauce and pour it over the chicken legs. Serve garnished with the lemon slices. *Serves 6-8.*

excellent (handwritten)

SWEET POTATOES WITH SAFFRON AND CINNAMON • Morroco

This Moroccan dish could be served at any American Thanksgiving. To substitute ½ teaspoon of dried ginger for the fresh is perfectly acceptable and more authentic. The Moroccans eat this at room temperature as a salad.*

2 large sweet potatoes (1 pound each)

1 teaspoon salt, or to taste

¼ teaspoon pepper, or to taste

1 pinch saffron threads soaked in 2 tablespoons hot water

1 tablespoon finely minced ginger

4 tablespoons sweet butter

1 tablespoon peanut or vegetable oil

½ teaspoon ground cinnamon

½ cup brown sugar

1 tablespoon minced parsley

Peel and cut each potato into 8 pieces. Add to a saucepan with all the rest of the ingredients except the parsley. Turn the heat to medium and cook, stirring gently until the butter melts. Then turn the heat to low, cover, and simmer for 20 minutes, stirring from time to time. (Don't worry, the potatoes will yield the necessary liquid.) When the potatoes are beginning to fall apart, cook until the sauce is syrupy.

Transfer to a small platter and serve garnished with the parsley. *Serves 4-6.*

* This recipe and the next are adapted from the English-language version of Lafita Bennani Smires' *Moroccan Cooking*, which I was fortunate to obtain from someone who purchased it in Morocco. To my knowledge, it is not widely available here, but for those with an interest in Moroccan cuisine it is worth tracking down (see BIBLIOGRAPHY).

KEFTA MEATBALLS WITH EGGS • Morocco

This authentic tajine* features finely chopped lamb, fragrant with herbs and spices, that is kneaded like bread and formed into marbles. It is cooked and served straight from the pot in its own rich sauce, topped with barely poached eggs. For those who like it hot, more cayenne may be added to the meat mixture or one or more dried hot peppers to the sauce. It is traditionally served with Middle Eastern bread, but is excellent with rice. The same meatballs may be grilled or broiled on skewers.

1½ pounds ground lamb (ask butcher to grind at least ¼ pound of pure fat with this mixture)

2 teaspoons cumin seeds

1 bunch parsley

1 bunch coriander

1 medium-sized onion

¼ teaspoon ground cayenne or other hot pepper powder

1 teaspoon salt, or to taste

2 teaspoons finely minced fresh ginger, or ½ teaspoon ground

3 teaspoons paprika

4½ tablespoons butter

6 eggs

Chopped coriander for garnish

Put the lamb in a mixing bowl. Toast the cumin seeds and rub them between your palms as you add them to the lamb. Chop the parsley, coriander, and onion and add to the lamb mixture along with the cayenne, salt, ginger, and 2 teaspoons of paprika. Blend the mixture well with your fingers, then transfer it to a cutting board and mince it still finer. Knead this mixture almost like bread dough for 3 minutes and leave to stand for 1 hour.

Form the meat into balls the size of marbles, wetting your hands often. Heat the butter in a heavy skillet over medium heat and saute lightly for 10 minutes, stirring from time to time. A sauce should be created from the meatball juices and the butter. Remove from the heat and allow to sit.

To finish, strain the sauce into a shallow heat-proof casserole. Sprinkle in the remaining teaspoon of paprika, and add the meatballs. Over low heat, stirring if necessary, bring the dish to a piping hot temperature.

Break the eggs gently into the casserole, evenly spaced on top of the meatballs. Cook until the whites are barely set.

Season with a little more salt if desired, then add the chopped coriander leaves and serve. *Serves 6.*

* See note, page 115.

GINGER SPREADS WEST

*Greeks, Romans, and
"The Plant of Zinj"*

*Medieval Europe and
the Spice Trade*

Gingerbread

*Modern Europe
and America*

Ginger in the West

J ust as in Asia, ginger was an important food and medicine in the West right from its introduction; but in the West it became a precious commodity as well. It was literally as good as gold during periods of Western history from the Roman Empire to Medieval Europe, when ships were dispatched in all directions in a race to control the profitable spice trade.

The Arabs introduced dried ginger to the ancient Greeks, and for centuries held on to the Western franchise for all Eastern spices by keeping the sources secret. It was the Western craze for dried ginger that led to its cultivation and use fresh for the first time outside its native Asia. By the late sixteenth century, fresh ginger was a food staple throughout the tropics. However, ginger's popularity as a spice began to fade in the West. "By the eighteenth century," according to Elizabeth David, "the ginger mania appears to have simmered down considerably...."[1] She speaks of England, but this phenomenon applied to the rest of Europe and Colonial America as well. Only very recently has fresh ginger become a feature of produce markets in Europe and the United States. Cooks on both continents who have used the dried spice as part of a faded tradition have begun to experiment with the fresh rhizome.

The Greeks

The ancient Greeks used ginger medicinally, apparently having little appreciation for its culinary virtues. Its powers to heal and to maintain health were heavily endorsed. Among those who prescribed ginger for the masses were the physicians Hippocrates, Dioscordes, and Galen. Ginger's new role in the West was not exactly new, however, but neither were the ideas of Western medicine. The Greek fathers outlined a theory of health based on a balance of heat and cold and of dampness and dryness that had more than casual links to Chinese medicine, where from its beginnings ginger was known as "the plant which repels dampness and wind."

The Romans

Where the Greeks seemed to use ginger because it was good for them, the Romans lusted after it. They devoured enormous quantities of spices, and especially relished the hot ones, pepper and ginger. (Unfortunately for the Romans, chili peppers were unknown in the Old World.) Besides perking up boiled ostrich or stuffed dormice, these spices were among the essential luxuries that were the basis of Rome's foreign trade.[2] In the first century A.D., over half the goods Rome imported from Asia and East Africa were classified as spices. The government reportedly earned substantial sums from a luxury tax imposed on ginger. Some citizens complained about its artificially high price; ginger, though more plentiful than black pepper, at one point sold for fifteen times as much.[3]

From what is known, Roman cooking did not take advantage of the culinary nuances of its many spices and herbs. Ginger was no exception. Roman writers detailed its medicinal qualities, but as a seasoning it was simply (and excitingly) hot to Roman tastes. There was little distinction made between ginger and pepper; in fact, people thought they came from the same source. Pliny the Elder wrote, "Many have taken ginger for the root of that tree [pepper]; but it is no so."[4] This confusion may explain the discrepancy in the call for ginger and pepper in a book of recipes compiled under the name of Apicius, the only comprehensive guide to the cooking of the Roman Empire. It contains only thirteen recipes using ginger, while nearly all call for pepper.

Ginger's Origins: A Mystery in the West

Before the first century A.D. most of the ginger that reached Greece and Rome came from India. By the second century, the bulk of it came by means of the famous "silk road" from China. But until the Romans actually found their way by ship to India in the first century A.D., ginger, in the form of shriveled little rhizomes, was an elixir of mysterious origin. Arab dealers kept the Westerners in the dark by concocting fantastic stories about the origins of all spices. The Greek authority Dioscordes wrote, "Ginger is a special kind of plant produced for the most part in Troglodytic Arabia."[5] Troglodytes, cited often in the literature of ancient Greece, were primitive cave and tunnel dwellers who lived along the Red Sea. They tatooed themselves, drank a mixture of milk and cattle blood, strangled their old when they could no longer tend animals, and achieved a reputation as robbers. It is doubtful that they grew ginger.

"The Plant of Zinj":
East Africa and Ethiopia

Evidence suggests that ginger has been cultivated and used fresh in coastal East Africa and Ethiopia since Greek and Roman times, perhaps before. This could explain the Greek notion that ginger was a product of Troglodytic Arabia. Most sources credit the Arabs with taking ginger from India and planting it in East Africa, but they may have found it growing there.

Intriguingly, there are elements in Ethiopian cooking, the use of fresh ginger being only one, that point to an early connection between Ethiopia and Java.[6] Ethiopia is an anomaly in ginger history. Ethiopians use fresh ginger, while the rest of North Africa uses it dried, and they apparently have done so for quite some time. It is possible that long ago fresh ginger made a 4,500-mile trip from Indonesia to East Africa. Trade between Southeast Asia and East Africa by outrigger canoe has a long history.

This would also explain how the Arabs, if they brought ginger to East Africa, could have written of ginger as a native plant. They called it the plant of Zinj (Arabic for *zanzibar* or Black Africa) or *zinjabil*, from which we get the word ginger directly via the Latin *zingiber*.*

---

* It is popularly reported that ginger comes from the Sanskrit *sringavera*, meaning "horn root." The Arabs, it is explained, came up with *zinjabil* by mistaking the meaning of the Sanskrit word when they encountered it. Scholars, however, doubt the existence of *sringavera*. Many feel it was made up after the fact to fill some etymological gaps.

Medieval Europe

Ginger was known in much of Europe and England, before the crusaders, who were responsible for bringing most other spices back from the wars. Elizabeth David supposes it reached England with the Romans. Ginger undoubtedly got a boost from Europe's first medical center, the famed school at Salerno. This school, established sometime in the seventh century, reached its peak of influence in the twelfth century and was to affect European diet and health for the next 500 years. The regimen of Salerno was based on Greek ideas, which in turn harked back to the very earliest notions of diet and health in China. Foremost among them was the concept of four humors—phlegm, blood, bile, and black bile—to be kept in balance for health. An excess of phlegm, characterized by cold and moisture, could be cured by a hot and dry food, such as ginger.

The spice craze began to soar by the fourteenth century, with ginger at the forefront. Everything was dosed with a familiar litany of spices, which included pepper and cinnamon. Ginger became a fixture on the table like salt and pepper. The *quatre-épices* mixture of today (pepper, ginger, cloves, nutmeg, sometimes cinnamon) used in sausages and terrines is a vestige of medieval meat preservation which used spices.* Other vestiges include the now meatless "minced-meat" pies, in which ginger, pepper, etc. were combined with meat and innards, raisins, currants, wine, or sherry. Roasted meats were never served without a spicy dipping sauce, and by the fourteenth century, sauce makers were familiar figures in Paris. Three sauces, which were the forerunners of condiments such as mustard and catsup, were popular: a yellow sauce, dominated by ginger and saffron; a green sauce, with ginger, cloves, cardamom, and fresh herbs; and a cinnamon sauce, *cameline*, which often contained more ginger than cinnamon.

* Jane Grigson, an authority on charcuterie, credits ginger's cousin galangal, widely used in the Middle Ages, as the base for the word "galantine."

Fresh ginger was available at one time in the Middle Ages in England, more widely available than it is today outside Oriental communities, according to food historian Karen Hess. It had to be to make the wildly popular candied ginger. Once sugar became plentiful, all sorts of fruits and herbs were used in making sweetmeats. Initially they were medicinal, and the sugar was to make them palatable. Of the most revered medicinals, ginger was the easiest to candy. On this score, there was little competition from peppercorns or cinnamon bark.

The Spice Trade

To link ginger to the grandeur of Venice is not as preposterous as it seems. It was the merchants of Venice who, after some clever dealings during the Crusades, got the first stranglehold on the European spice trade that was to last until the fifteenth century. As Elizabeth David tells us, "Who knows which palaces, now crumbling to their ruin on the Grand Canal, were indirectly subsidized by the spice-hungry English."[7] As she later points out, the spice-hungry English were in large measure the ginger-hungry English.

The Venetians bought their spices at Alexandria and Damascus—some 5,000 tons annually, half of which were ginger and pepper. When Marco Polo encountered ginger in China, he was amazed at its price—next to nothing by Venetian standards. Upon reaching Venice, ginger was as good as currency. In fact, a pound each of ginger, pepper, and cinnamon was demanded annually of Venetian merchants by their master of the treasury in order to let their goods enter Europe without the usual red tape.

In the fifteenth century, the Venetians lost their grip on the spice trade as the Spanish and Portuguese set sail. Ginger was introduced to Jamaica and the New World on the heels of Columbus' first voyages. By 1547, it was a cash crop shipped regularly back to Spain. Meanwhile, the Portuguese had reached the real Indies (India). In 1498, Vasco de Gama struck a deal with the ruler of Calicut—ginger, pepper, cinnamon, and cloves could be had for mere silver and gold. The Portuguese began growing their own ginger in West Africa and Brazil, and the Africans they enslaved in both places began using fresh ginger in their cooking.

West Africa and the New World

The Cookery of Slaves

Ginger was one of several cash crops introduced by Spain and Portugal into their newly appropriated lands in the sixteenth century. Ginger industries set up by the Spanish in Jamaica and by the Portuguese in Sierra Leone are still going strong. Other native Asian foods, such as bananas, sugar cane, and citrus, have not fared badly either. The Europeans did not hire people to tend their crops; they used slaves, who were put to work by the millions in the West Indies, Brazil, and their native West Africa.

The slaves made the first new use of fresh ginger in centuries, creating exciting dishes from the marriage of Old and New World foods. Using the peanuts, tomatoes, and chilis of the New World and their own native palm oil, coconut, and dried shrimp, they concocted rich sauces for fish and poultry. Fresh ginger added a refreshing balance to these peanut sauces, as it would later when the peanut found its way to Southeast Asia. Ginger was paired with African yams and New World corn and avocados for the first time.

With the abundance of sugar cane, sweet dishes were created using fresh ginger, coconut, rum, and the vanilla bean. The "new natives" of the West Indies, aware of ginger's medicinal powers, brewed a simple ginger tea for stomach ailments.

Fresh ginger today is used throughout Africa, with the exception of the Moslem north, where it is used dried and ground. In Africa, people of European descent depend on it dried or preserved, though Indian cooks, of which there are many, use it fresh. The use of fresh ginger has spread throughout the West Indies, Brazil, and elsewhere in Latin America. In Central America, it is cultivated for export as well as for the local market. To the best of my knowledge, ginger in any form is rarely used in Mexican cooking, though it is one of their herbal medicines.

123

NOTES—GINGER SPREADS WEST

1. Elizabeth David, *Spices, Salts and Aromatics in the English Kitchen*, Penguin, 1981, p. 34
2. Reay Tannahill, *Food in History*, 1973, p. 103
3. Waverly Root, *Food*, 1980, p. 148
4. Henry Yule and A. C. Burnell, *Hobson-Jobson: A Glossary of Colloquial Anglo-Indian Words*, 1903-updated, p. 374
5. Laurens van der Post, *African Cooking*, 1970
6. Tannahill, p. 219
7. David, p. 9

SQUID AND SHRIMP SALAD · *West African Style*

This simple-to-make dish of poached squid and shrimp can, and in fact should, be made ahead of time. It is best if it sits for 15 to 30 minutes.

1 pound fresh squid, cleaned, cut, and scored as in Squid with Black Beans, Chilis, and Young Ginger, page 62.

1 pound medium-sized shrimp, shelled, deveined, and cut in half lengthwise

2 teaspoons minced ginger

2 teaspoons minced garlic

2 tomatoes, peeled, seeded, and diced

½ cup red onion, finely chopped

5-10 fresh red chilis, cut into ½-inch cubes

¼ cup green bell pepper, cut into ½-inch cubes

¼ cup chopped parsley or fresh coriander

⅓ cup fresh lime juice

¼ cup olive oil

1 teaspoon salt, or to taste

1 teaspoon black pepper

Bring a generous amount of water to a boil in a large pot. Add the squid and shrimp, stirring to separate the pieces. Cook for 30 seconds, drain, and run immediately under cold water until cool. Drain well. About 30 minutes before serving, combine the remaining ingredients with the squid and shrimp. Serve the salad at room temperature, tossing just before serving. *Serves 4-6.*

The Peanut Sauces of
Africa and Brazil

Among the more visible evidence of the slave trade's impact on world cuisine is the intriguing genre of peanut stews of West Africa that manifest themselves in the *vatapa* dishes of Brazil. Africans are thought to have originated these dishes in their homeland from South America's peanuts, tomatoes, and chili peppers, which were introduced to West Africa by the Portuguese. When West African slaves were shipped to Brazil by the Portuguese, the captives brought their recipes with them. The main ingredients of these stews are usually seafood or poultry, but they may include pork and, in Brazil, turkey as well. The indigenous cashew nut may replace the peanut in some Brazilian versions.

PEANUT STEW WITH CHICKEN AND CONDIMENTS • West Africa

The variation of peanut stew that follows was inspired by a recipe in Time-Life's African cookbook. It is a meal in itself, with six exotic condiments. For the purposes of this book, it illustrates exciting uses of fresh and ground ginger typical of West Africa. Both are used in the main dish, and, among the condiments, fresh ginger is paired with avocado, and ground ginger combines with fried plantains. The okra that cooks with the dish at the end is native to Africa and has long had spiritual significance, as it now does among West African sects in Brazil.

    This dish is ideal for dinner guests; it may be prepared ahead, and it is unusual. As with the *vatapa* recipe that follows, it need only be accompanied by rice and a simple vegetable or salad, and is more flavorful if the nut butter, either peanut or cashew, is blended rather than bought.*

---

* To make your own peanut butter: Heat 2 cups of peanut oil in a wok or saucepan until nearly smoking. Turn off the heat and add 1 cup of raw peanuts, and let cook until golden brown. Remove to drain with a slotted spoon, reserving the oil for another use. The peanuts may be blended into a rough-textured paste in a food processor or blender. The alternative is to use any brand of natural peanut butter.

1 large chicken, 5 to 6 pounds, or
   2 small chickens 2½ to 3 pounds
   each, cut (bones and all) into a total
   of 10 or more pieces

1 tablespoon salt

1 tablespoon ground ginger

½ cup peanut oil

6 or more small dried chili peppers

1 cup coarsely chopped onion

2 tablespoons minced fresh ginger

2 tablespoons minced fresh garlic

6 small red or green chilis, minced

2 cups peeled, seeded, and chopped ripe
   tomatoes (or canned Italian plum
   tomatoes)

½ cup tiny dried shrimp, finely ground
   in food processor, mortar, or blender

1 teaspoon white pepper

6 cups boiling water

1 cup peanut butter

12 whole fresh okra

6 to 8 small hard-boiled eggs

Coat the chicken pieces with the salt and ground ginger, and set aside. Prepare the garnishes as described below and set aside in small attractive serving bowls.

Heat the oil in a large, heavy skillet and brown the chicken pieces in two batches. Remove with a slotted spoon and drain. Add the dried chili peppers and the onions to the same oil and cook, stirring, scraping the brown particles stuck to the bottom of the pan, until the onions are translucent.

Add the fresh ginger, garlic, and fresh chilis and stir for 15 seconds longer; then add the tomatoes, dried shrimp and white pepper and stir briefly to blend. Add one cup of the boiling water and the peanut butter. Cook, stirring, until well blended. Add more water if necessary. Return the chicken pieces to the sauce, stirring to coat.

Add the remaining water and stir to blend. When piping hot, turn the heat to low and cook covered for 30 minutes, stirring from time to time to prevent sticking. Add the okra and cook for another 30 minutes, stirring frequently. Add the hard-boiled eggs for the last 5 minutes to reheat. Serve on a large platter, surrounded by the condiments. *Serves 6-8.*

Condiments

AVOCADO WITH FRESH GINGER
Chop one large ripe avocado into cubes of ½ inch or less and combine with 1 tablespoon of freshly squeezed lemon juice, 1½ teaspoons finely minced fresh ginger, and ½ teaspoon salt.

FRIED PEANUTS
Deep-fry raw peanuts in the same oil used to fry the plantains, let cool, then chop coarsely.

TOMATOES/ONIONS/FRESH CORIANDER

Peel and chop 2 large ripe tomatoes, and mix with ½ cup of chopped onion, two tablespoons of chopped fresh coriander, ½ teaspoon cayenne or other dried chili pepper powder, 1 tablespoon freshly squeezed lemon juice, and ½ teaspoon salt.

PAPAYA WITH GREEN CHILIS

Peel, seed, and dice a ¾-pound ripe papaya into ½-inch cubes, and blend with one hot green chili (finely chopped seeds, and all), and 1 tablespoon of lemon juice.

FRIED PLANTAIN CUBES

Peel and dice two medium-sized plantains and deep-fry in one cup of peanut oil until golden brown. Drain and toss with ¼ teaspoon ground ginger, ¼ teaspoon of ground dried chilis or cayenne, and ¼ teaspoon salt.

DICED PINEAPPLE

Cut fresh ripe pineapple into ½-inch cubes, until you have a cup or so.

VATAPA (Fish and Shrimp in Ginger-Cashew Sauce) • Brazil

Variations of *vatapa* abound in the Bahia region of Brazil, where people have African roots. A whole fish smothered with a sauce of cashew nuts and coconut, not to mention a pound of fresh shrimp, renders the dish a spectacular centerpiece to any meal.

1 white-fleshed fish, 2½ to 3 pounds (for visual appeal, an East Coast red snapper or a West Coast red rock cod of high grade is recommended)

1 pound shrimp, shelled, deveined, and cut in half lengthwise

Salt

1 cup peanut oil

¾ cup raw cashews

½ cup dried shrimp

2 cups peeled, seeded, and chopped ripe tomatoes (or canned Italian plum tomatoes)

1 can unsweetened coconut milk (about 14 ounces), or 1½ cups fresh

1 cup milk

½ cup finely chopped fresh coriander leaves and stems

1 cup finely chopped onion

2 tablespoons minced fresh ginger

3 or more hot green chili peppers, finely chopped, seeds and all

¼ cup dende oil (optional)*

½ teaspoon freshly ground black pepper, or more to taste

Sprigs of fresh coriander for garnish

* For those not near a Latin American market, ¼ cup of olive oil mixed with 1 teaspoon paprika is a vague substitute.

Rinse the fish inside and out, pat dry, and set aside. Toss the fresh shrimp in 1 teaspoon of salt and set aside. Heat the oil in a heavy saucepan to near smoking, add the cashews, and turn off the heat. Allow to cook until lightly browned, then remove to a food processor, blender, or heavy mortar, and blend with the dried shrimp to a smooth paste. Add this to a bowl with tomatoes, coconut milk, and milk. In another bowl, combine the coriander, onion, ginger, and chilis, and set aside.

Reheat the oil to hot and add the shrimp, stirring to separate. Cook just until they change color, then remove and drain. Pour half the oil into a skillet large enough to fit the fish. Heat the oil and the onion mixture, and cook until the onion turns translucent, but don't let it brown. Keeping aside the pepper and *dende* oil, add the remaining sauce ingredients, and 1½ teaspoons salt, or to taste. Bring the mixture to a boil, stir it, reduce the heat, and simmer for 5 minutes. Turn up the heat and add the fish. When it boils, reduce to a simmer and allow to cook for 10 minutes. Turn the fish over and cook for another 10 minutes. Carefully remove it to a large serving platter, leaving the sauce in the pan.

Stir the sauce and turn up the heat slightly. Reheat the shrimp in the sauce. Add the *dende* oil, if using, and sprinkle with the black pepper. Pour this sauce over the fish and serve garnished with the coriander sprigs. *Serves 6-8.*

BRAISED DUCK WITH ORANGE AND CLOVES • *East Africa*

This recipe, of Zanzibar origin, is close in its method of cooking to the delicious duck casseroles of China. The clove/fresh ginger/citrus combination works wonderfully with this rich bird. (Zanzibar is the leading producer of cloves.)

1 fresh duck (about 5 pounds)

1 tablespoon salt

2 cups or more vegetable oil for browning the duck

10 red chili peppers, shredded

2 tablespoons or more finely shredded fresh ginger

2 tablespoons finely shredded lime peel, with white part carefully removed

6 smashed garlic cloves

1 cup thinly sliced onions

3 cups chicken stock, fresh or canned

15 whole cloves

2 teaspoons of salt, or less if you use canned chicken stock

1 cup freshly squeezed orange juice

¼ cup sugar

½ teaspoon freshly ground white pepper

10 to 12 thin slices of orange, cut in half, for garnish

Rinse and dry the duck thoroughly. Sprinkle the salt all over the duck, inside and out and allow to sit in a cool airy place for 4 hours or overnight. It's best to hang the duck, as the Chinese do.

Attach a string to the duck for easy maneuvering in the oil—either around the neck, if you buy a duck with the head on, or in a long loop at the base of both wings, which will make a sort of string handle.

Heat the oil in a large heavy skillet (a wok is best for this, since there is no way to avoid some sputtering of the hot oil). Gently lower the duck into the hot oil, using the string and a metal spatula. Spoon the oil over the duck for 7 to 8 minutes; then remove the duck carefully in a horizontal position, and drain away any liquid that has accumulated in the cavity. Turn the duck over and return to the oil to brown on the other side. Repeat the browning and spooning the oil over the duck for another 7 to 8 minutes. Remove and drain.

Drain all but about 3 tablespoons of the oil from the pan, then heat the pan over a high flame. Add the shredded red chilis, the fresh ginger shreds, the lime peel, the garlic cloves, and the onions, and cook, stirring, for 2 minutes until the onions are translucent, and just starting to brown.

Add the remaining ingredients and bring to a boil. Then add the duck. Turn the heat to medium-low and simmer the duck, covered, for 2 hours, turning from time to time. If the liquid cooks away, adjust the heat and add more water.

When the duck is done, transfer it to a serving platter, leaving the sauce in the pan. Turn the heat to high and cook the sauce until it thickens. Pour over the duck and garnish the platter with the orange slices. *Serves 4-6.*

PICADILLO WITH DEEP-FRIED EGGS • *Cuba*

A little of this rich, spiced meat dish goes a long way. The beef is cooked slowly until it falls apart into shreds. The textures and tastes of ginger, garlic, olives, raisins, and olive oil combine wonderfully. Chilis and black pepper cut the richness. The particularly Cuban addition of deep-fried eggs (actually eggs poached in oil) is an unusual and delicious touch.

Picadillo is versatile, and may be used as a stuffing for peppers to be broiled or grilled, or a tasty filling for a sandwich made with fresh Cuban bread. It may also be served over rice. It makes a good buffet dish, as it reheats well.

1 cup olive oil

4 pounds good beef chuck, cut into 2-inch cubes

½ cup chopped garlic

¼ cup chopped fresh ginger

2 teaspoons freshly ground black pepper

3 teaspoons salt, or to taste

1½ cups chopped onions

½ cup chopped chilis, red or green

4 large sweet peppers, red or green, chopped

3 cups chopped canned Italian plum tomatoes

½ teaspoon ground cloves

1 cinnamon stick

½ cup pitted and chopped green olives

⅓ cup seeded raisins

¼ cup freshly squeezed lime juice

Peanut or vegetable oil

7 small eggs

Sprigs of fresh coriander for garnish

Heat ½ cup olive oil in a large heavy skillet, and brown the beef chunks a pound at a time, removing them with a slotted spoon. When beef is browned, return to the skillet and toss with the garlic, ginger, and pepper. Add boiling water to cover and 2 teaspoons of salt.

Turn the heat to low and simmer, stirring and checking from time to time to make sure there is enough liquid. After 1½ hours, the meat should start to fall apart, and there should be very little liquid left. If not, raise the heat and cook, stirring, until most of the liquid is gone. Meanwhile, heat the remaining oil in another skillet. Add the onions, chilis and sweet peppers and cook, stirring, until the onions are translucent. Add the tomatoes, cloves, cinnamon stick, and 1 teaspoon salt. Cook until most of the liquid has evaporated, and set aside until the beef is ready.

When the beef is falling apart, reheat the onion-pepper mixture and add the olives, raisins, and lime juice. Stir mixture into the beef, check the seasonings, transfer to a large serving platter and keep warm, while preparing the eggs.

Heat 1 inch of oil in a skillet. Gently slide in the eggs and cook over low heat until the whites are set and the yolks are still runny, about 2 to 3 minutes. With a slotted spoon remove the eggs to the top of the picadillo. Garnish with coriander and serve. *Serves 8-10.*

GINGER MOUSSE • *West Indies*

This excellent creamy custard comes from Trinidad, and the ginger and rum seem to have a special affinity for one another. The version below was adapted from two recipes that called for preserved ginger.* This recipe uses fresh ginger and adds heavy cream, to a delicious end.

4 tablespoons water

1 envelope, or 1 tablespoon, plain gelatin

1 cup heavy cream

1 can evaporated milk (13 ounces)

6 egg yolks

9 tablespoons sugar

¼ cup finely minced fresh ginger

½ cup rum

5 egg whites

¼ teaspoon salt

Pour the water into the top of a small double boiler and sprinkle in the gelatin. Let it sit for a couple of minutes, then turn on the heat and stir the gelatin over the simmering water until it dissolves. Turn off the heat and cover the double boiler.

Combine the cream and evaporated milk in an enamel, glass, or stainless steel saucepan and heat until bubbles form around the edges. Remove from heat.

Beat the egg yolks until well blended, then gradually add all but a tablespoon of the sugar, beating constantly. Continue to beat the mixture until it makes a ribbon as it falls from the beater.

Don't stop. Continue to beat the yolks while adding the milk in a thin stream. Transfer the mixture to a saucepan, and stir over a low heat until it thickens enough to coat a spoon. Be patient. Don't let the custard boil, or it will curdle. When good and thick, stir in the gelatin and the ginger; pour the mixture into a large mixing bowl, scraping out every tasty drop with a spatula. Warm the rum in a pan and ignite it. Shake the pan back and forth gently until the flame goes out, then stir it into the custard. Let the custard cool. (To speed up the process, set the mixing bowl in a larger bowl of cold water or cracked ice and stir until the custard is cool.) Set aside.

Beat the egg whites until frothy in a separate bowl. Add the final tablespoon of sugar and the salt and beat until the whites form stiff peaks. Gently fold the egg whites into the custard mixture, and continue to stir them carefully until well mixed. Chill, covered, in individual dishes or a serving bowl until firm, at least 3 hours. *Serves 6-8.*

* Recipes for ginger mousse from Elisabeth Lambert Ortiz's fine work on Caribbean cookery, and *The Cooking of the Caribbean Islands*, Time-Life Books.

TROPICAL FRUITS AND RASPBERRIES WITH COCONUT CREAM SAUCE

This combination was inspired by the succulent fruits of the West Indies, West Africa, and Southeast Asia. The sauce could work with a variety of fruits.

1 perfectly ripe pineapple

2 ripe mangoes

2 ripe bananas

1 pint fresh raspberries

2 teaspoons finely minced fresh ginger
  (preferably young ginger)

2 tablespoons lime juice

1 tablespoon sugar

1 cup coconut cream (an 8-ounce can)

1 pint of whipping cream

Cube the pineapple and the mangoes. Slice the bananas in half lengthwise and cut into 1-inch lengths. Toss all the fruit, including the raspberries, with the ginger, lime juice, and sugar, and transfer to a serving bowl.

Blend the coconut cream, which tends to separate in the can. Whip the heavy cream until just thick and fold into the coconut cream.

Serve the fruit with the sauce on the side, allowing people to help themselves to the sauce. *Serves 6-8.*

BANANA CARAMEL · Brazil

Here is an unusual spiced confection, served in small slices with coffee. It is important that the bananas be fully ripe—soft and strong-flavored, with skin that is blackening.

2 pounds bananas

1 pound dark brown sugar*

¼ cup minced fresh ginger

1 teaspoon cinnamon

Mash the bananas thoroughly and blend well with the other ingredients. (This may be done in a food processor.) Cook this mixture in a heavy skillet over a low flame, stirring constantly to keep it from burning, until the mixture is deep brown and begins to form a cohesive mass. (To test the mixture, drop a tiny spoonful into a bowl of ice water; it should form a soft ball.) When it reaches this stage, remove the candy to an oiled plate and allow it to cool somewhat. Mold it into a small loaf with the back of a spoon. Allow to cool thoroughly and serve in thin slices. *Makes 1 small (2- by 6-inch) loaf.*

* Brazilians favor dark brown sugar, which gives a powerful molasses flavor. For a lighter caramel, substitute white sugar.

GINGER
BREAD

Gingerbread

I initially approached this chapter as an obligation. Everyone knows something about gingerbread, and the association between ginger and gingerbread is so close that I was determined to drive a wedge between them. When I began to research gingerbread, however, I became engrossed, and discovered that gingerbread is a book-sized subject unto itself. It plays a fascinating part in the traditions of all the countries of Europe, as well as the United States.

This also became the chapter where I was the most ill at ease with the recipes; putting together a bread and pastry section unnerved me. Give me a Chinese cleaver, some strange vegetation, and a dozen weird shellfish, and I feel relaxed, but I run from a baking pan. I was overjoyed when several of the Bay Area's notable pastry experts agreed to bring a carefully selected variety of gingerbreads and their recipes to a tasting. What could have been the least interesting recipes in the book turned out to be a uniquely fine sampling of gingerbreads.

Gingerbread entails the convergence of two distinct ancestral lines, one of which sprang from England, the other, the more significant one, from Germany.

English Gingerbrati and Gyngerbrede

The word "gingerbread" can be traced to *gingerbrati*, which were medicinal ginger pastes. In the early thirteenth century England, these were well known to the apothecaries in the form of electuaries—medicated hard candies that had nothing to do with bread or baking. A popular formula called for ginger, galangal, pepper, nutmeg, honey, and parsnips.[1] Over the next century these medicinals came to be called "gyngerbrede," and breadcrumbs were used in place of starchy roots. "Gyngerbrede" was still not a true bread by any stretch of the imagination, but was rather, in the terminology of the times, a dry "leach," meaning something that could be sliced. This was the gingerbread of England until the early seventeenth century, when French and German bakers introduced the more familiar modern version using flour and eggs. A particularly English confection continued to evolve, however, with molasses from England's colonies replacing honey. The rest of Europe stuck with honey or later incorporated refined sugar into its recipes.

German Gingerbread and French Pain d'Épice

The origin of the notorious gingerbread man is often credited to the court of Queen Elizabeth I, where important visitors were presented with charming likenesses of themselves in gingerbread. But it was more likely in Germany where the first such use of gingerbread took place. Long before Elizabeth, German bakers were creating works of art from gingerbread. They are thought to have adapted the spiced honey cakes of the Middle East that they encountered during the Crusades.[2]

Nuremberg, to this day, reigns as the gingerbread capital of the world. Soon after the Crusades it became a center of the spice trade, as tons of ginger, pepper, and cinnamon came over the Alps from Venice. The lush forests surrounding the city were soon filled with beekeepers, who supplied the honey for these confections.

From Germany the passion for gingerbread spread to Strasbourg and Rheims, where *pain d'épice* became synonymous with the finest of the baker's art. Gingerbread's medicinal beginnings were not forgotten, at least by Nicholas Abraham, doctor to Louis XIII, who wrote in 1608, "the women, of Rheims [because of] the ordinary use of this bread, are rendered beautiful and have a beautiful color and a robust and succulent body."[3]

The intricately sculptured gingerbread molds from this period, which are now collector's items, give us a unique glimpse into the life and times of medieval Europe. Each nation had its artisans and their creations spanned the esthetic styles of the age, from the Gothic to the Baroque, etc. Gingerbread makers were recognized as artists rather than cooks, and guilds were established that separated the bakers of *pain d'épice* from the bakers of day-to-day breads. Germany's gingerbread makers were established by the fourteenth century; the *pain d'épiciers* organized in Rheims in 1571. By that time, the art of gingerbread was spreading all over Europe. Poland enjoyed its first *piernik* in the fourteenth century; Hungary took it up in the fifteenth century; and Czechoslovakia and Russia, perhaps, in the sixteenth century. In Russia, at the birth of Peter the Great, a variety of gingerbreads were ceremoniously presented, including a gingerbread Kremlin that is reported to have weighed between 150 and 200 pounds.

The Tradition of Gingerbread

The first gingerbread artisans catered to the aristocracy. Detailed molds were sculpted from hardwood depicting everyday scenes from the lives of the rich—nobles in full regalia, women at their toilette, fancy horse-drawn carriages about to set forth on an errand, etc. The market expanded in the seventeenth century to include the wealthy bourgeois, and the subject matter of the molds expanded as well. For the first time there were scenes appropriate for the major religious days: St. Nicolas, Christmas, and Easter.

By the eighteenth century, little gingerbreads were selling like hot dogs or souvenirs at fairs and carnivals, as they found their way into the daily lives and small celebrations of everyone. Their themes were focused to appeal to every village and town—for example, coats of arms and insignias of the local militia. Religious themes were expanded. Poland took this even a step further, with images of peasant life. There were gingerbread chickens, dogs, storks, bears, and serfs.

Gingerbread took on the function of greeting cards during the Romantic Age. There were edible Christmas cards with gaily colored piped-sugar pictures of angels, doves, and other favorites. The German *lebkuchen* heart, with counterparts throughout Europe, became the most important lover's gift, baked with inscriptions and affixed with a small mirror. Until World War II these *pains d'amorieux* were popular in Alsace, and the practice of exchanging gingerbread hearts is still carried on in Yugoslavia.

The spice breads of the nineteenth century lost their fine details because they were stamped out rather than molded. There are still vestiges of the earlier tradition to be found in the *couques* of Dinant in Belgium, the gingerbreads of Wagner's Ring Cycle sold in Bayreuth, and the *speculatius* family of pastries found in Vienna and throughout Belgium and Holland.

Americans carried on the tradition of gingerbread, and added their own touches.[4] Soft cake-like breads became popular—leavened with pearl ash, a homemade forerunner of bicarbonate of soda and the various baking powders that came later. Gingerbreads, gingerbread men, cookies, and snaps (one of the earlier and most successful commercially baked goods) are part of our cooking heritage and are one of the noteworthy features of American cuisine.

NOTES—GINGERBREAD

1. A proposition of Karen Hess in her annotations of *Martha Washington's Booke of Cookery* (BIBLIOGRAPHY).
2. French experts, tracing their own distinguished *pain d'épice*, acknowledge this route to Germany, but attribute all to an ancient Chinese honey bread known as *mi-kong*, which was rationed to the followers of Ghengis Khan.
3. "The Government Necessary to Each," via *Le Pain*, Bernard Dupaigne.
4. According to Waverly Root, one of the touches was the use of ginger cookies to direct the choice of voters for the House of Burgesses in early Virginia.

GINGER HONEY CAKE • *Middle East*

Alan Oswald, who makes a number of delectable baked goods at his Alano's Pastries in Walnut Creek, California, contributed this cake made entirely with rye flour in the style of the Middle East. He makes these with nutmeg, anise, and cardamom, but this one has a decidedly non-Middle Eastern touch—minced fresh ginger.

4¾ cups medium rye flour

1 teaspoon nutmeg

1½ teaspoons baking powder

1¼ teaspoons baking soda

1¼ teaspoons salt

1¼ cup raisins, lightly chopped

1¾ cups honey

½ cup peanut or corn oil

1 cup whole eggs

1¼ cups milk

¼ cup finely minced fresh ginger

Sift together, twice, the rye flour, nutmeg, baking powder, baking soda, and salt, and set aside. Combine the raisins, honey, oil, and eggs; mix well and add to the flour mixture. Add the milk and ginger, and mix until well blended, scraping the bowl as you stir. Cover the batter and hold it at room temperature for 1 hour.

Preheat the oven to 350°F. Grease three 7- by 2-inch round cake pans or three 4- by 8-inch loaf pans, and divide the batter among them. Place a shallow pan of hot water on the bottom oven rack, to be removed after 30 minutes. Put the three loaf pans in the oven and bake for about 50 minutes. *Makes 3 loaves.*

PAIN D'ÉPICE · Dijon

Lindsey Shere, who is in charge of pastries and desserts at Chez Panisse restaurant in Berkeley, contributed this truly wonderful French spice bread. It has its roots in Dijon in the Middle Ages. Like many other fine foods, it improves if it is aged for a few days—if you can wait.

1 cup hot water
1 cup honey
1 tablespoon sugar
¼ teaspoon salt
2 teaspoons baking soda
1 teaspoon baking powder
¼ cup rum
1½ teaspoons ground anise seeds
1 teaspoon ground cinnamon
¾ teaspoon ground ginger

¼ teaspoon ground cloves
Grating of white pepper
2 cups rye flour
1½ cups white flour
1 teaspoon grated orange rind
1 cup chopped almonds
3 tablespoons chopped candied clementine peel*
1½ tablespoons chopped candied angelica (optional)

Preheat the oven to 400°F.

Pour the hot water over the honey in a large bowl. Add the sugar, salt, baking soda, and baking powder. Stir to dissolve and blend. Add the rum and spices and a cup each of the rye and white flours and stir until blended. Add the rest of the flour and stir until smooth. Add the orange rind, almonds, candied peel, and angelica. Stir just until thoroughly blended, taking care not to overmix.

Liberally butter two loaf pans (4- by 8-inch or smaller), and fill them three-quarters full with the batter, spreading it evenly. Put the pans on the middle shelf of the oven and bake for 10 minutes. Reduce the heat to 350°F and continue to bake for an hour or until a toothpick inserted in the center comes out clean. Turn out onto a rack to cool when done. When completely cool, wrap the breads in foil or plastic wrap and allow to age a few days before eating. *Pain d'épice* will keep refrigerated for several weeks. Serve the bread thinly sliced with butter and tea or wine. In an emergency it may be eaten after it comes out of the oven, and it will still be delicious. *Makes 2 loaves.*

* Candied tangerine or orange peel could substitute for the clementine. The candied angelica may be omitted if not available.

SPECULAAS · Holland

Speculaas is an exquisite spiced pastry traditionally cut into thin cookie shapes or pressed into small wooden molds. This gingerbread has a long history, and classic variations are enjoyed in Holland, Belgium, and Austria. A very fine version can also be found in Oakland, California, where every December it is made by Karen Shapiro at her La Viennoise pastry shop. *Speculaas* is a specialty of Karen's, and she generously shared the recipe. It is well worth the effort to make and is both elegant and delicious.

Almond Paste Filling:

1 pound almond paste (available at specialty shops)

3 tablespoons apricot jam

⅓ cup honey

Gingerbread Dough:

5 cups pastry flour

2 teaspoons ground cinnamon

¾ teaspoon ground nutmeg

¾ teaspoon ground ginger

¾ teaspoon ground cloves

¼ teaspoon ground cardamom

¼ teaspoon finely ground white pepper

2¼ teaspoons baking powder

1¼ cups sweet butter

1 cup granulated sugar

¾ teaspoon salt

1 egg

Egg wash (1 egg yolk blended with 2 tablespoons water)

3 dozen whole blanched almonds

Mix the almond paste, together with the jam and the honey, to a smooth paste. Refrigerate overnight.

Combine the flour, spices, baking powder, butter, sugar, and salt in a large mixing bowl, and work together as you would a pie dough, until crumbly, about the texture of coarse corn meal. Add the egg and mix it well with the dough. Knead the dough a little, until all ingredients are well combined.

Have an ungreased 11- by 17-inch sheet pan ready and a large work space for rolling dough. Divide the dough in half. Roll out the first half until it is the size of the sheet tray, as best you can, and carefully transfer it to the tray. Roll out the almond paste filling until it is the same size, and cover the dough in the sheet tray with it. Repeat the procedure with the second half of the dough, which will form the top layer of the *speculaas.*

Preheat the oven to 350°F. Brush the top of the uncooked *speculaas* with the egg wash, which will glaze it when it is cooked. Garnish with the blanched almonds. Bake until golden brown, about 40 minutes. While the *speculaas* is still warm, cut it with a sharp knife into 33 rectangles of about 1½-by 3½-inches (three widths by eleven lengths of the sheet tray). When cool, remove and serve however you like. *Makes 33 pieces.*

MOLASSES GINGERBREAD • From American Cookery *by Amelia Simmons (1796)*

Marion Cunningham, author of the *Fannie Farmer Baking Book*, edited and tested this gingerbread created by Amelia Simmons, who described herself as "an American orphan" and who wrote *American Cookery*, the first American cookbook. This was one of five gingerbread recipes in *American Cookery*, a very slim volume, which is some indication of how beloved gingerbread was in eighteenth-century America. The original recipe appears below and, lest you have trouble following it, Marion's edited version follows. The pearl ash in the first recipe is potassium bicarbonate, which American women made at home from fireplace ashes. It was later replaced by baking soda.

"One tablespoon of cinnamon, one spoonful ginger, some coriander or alspice, put to four teaspoons pearl ash, dissolved in half pint of water, four pound flour, one quart molasses, six ounces butter, if in summer rub in the butter, if in the winter, warm the butter and molasses, and pour to the spiced flour . . . knead well till stiff, the more the better, the lighter and whiter it will be; bake brisk fifteen minutes; don't scorch; before it is put in, wash it with whites and sugar beat together."

½ cup butter, softened

½ cup dark molasses

2 cups all-purpose flour

1 tablespoon ground ginger

1 teaspoon ground cinnamon

2 teaspoons ground coriander

½ teaspoon salt

1 teaspoon baking soda, dissolved in 2 tablespoons hot water

¾ cup cold water

¼ cup granulated sugar to sprinkle on top of batter

Preheat oven to 375°F. Grease and lightly flour an 8- by 8-inch baking pan.

Combine the butter and molasses in a large mixing bowl and beat until well mixed. In a small bowl, mix together the flour, ginger, cinnamon, coriander, and salt, stirring with a fork to blend. Stir into the butter mixture. Beat well. Add the baking soda dissolved in water, stir and blend. Beat in the cold water and mix well. Spoon into the pan and sprinkle the sugar on top. Bake for about 20 minutes or until an inserted toothpick comes out clean. *Makes one 8- by 8-inch pan.*

GEORGE WASHINGTON'S MOTHER'S GINGERBREAD

Mary Ball Washington was supposed to have served this cake to the Marquis de Lafayette in 1784 when the Frenchman stopped by to see her son, George. She made him a mint julep to go with it. It is the most heavily spiced of the gingerbreads in this section and is quite tasty. Helen Gustafson, who works at the Chez Panisse Café in Berkeley, collects American gingerbread recipes, and contributed this to the book. Helen's kitchen, I might add, with its spice cupboard and baking cabinet, with built-in flour sifter from the nineteenth century, is the best possible place to make gingerbreads and drink tea.

½ cup butter

½ cup dark brown sugar

½ cup molasses

½ cup golden syrup

½ cup warm milk

2 tablespoons ground ginger

1½ teaspoons ground cinnamon

1½ teaspoons mace

1½ teaspoons grated nutmeg

¼ cup sherry

1 teaspoon cream of tartar

3 cups flour

3 well-beaten eggs

Juice and grated rind of 1 large orange

1 teaspoon baking soda dissolved in 2 tablespoons warm water

1 cup sultanas or raisins

Preheat the oven to 350°F.

In a mixing bowl, cream the butter and the sugar until well blended. Add the molasses, syrup, milk, spices, and sherry. Mix very well. Mix the cream of tartar with the flour and sift, a little at a time, into the butter and sugar mixture, adding alternately with the beaten eggs. Stir as you go. Add the orange juice and rind, the baking soda liquid, and the raisins. Mix to combine and pour into a well-greased 12- by 9- by 3-inch baking pan, and bake for 45 minutes, or until an inserted toothpick comes out clean. *Makes one 12- by 9-inch pan.*

San Francisco Victorian Gingerbread House – Jim Dodge

SAN FRANCISCO VICTORIAN GINGERBREAD HOUSE

Jim Dodge, the acclaimed young chef at the Stanford Court Hotel in San Francisco, created an elegant version of the traditional gingerbread house. His subject, quite appropriately, is the Victorian house as it is found throughout San Francisco. The decorative trim on Victorian houses came to be known as gingerbread, since it was eye-catching and served no function, just as the real gingerbread used for elaborate confectionary constructions was purely decorative and often too dense to eat. Jim made his house, however, so that people would want to pull pieces from it to pop in their mouths. His is hard to resist, with its chocolate-almond shingles and hazelnut sablés for windows and doors, but one hesitates to start tearing at a work of art.

The recipe below is the basic one Jim Dodge made. The confection is held together with royal icing (see below), and Jim suggests adding to his design however you please—candy canes, gum drops, etc. You may also want to alter the size and the shape of the house according to your own whim. In this case it is recommended that you make a plan, with cardboard cutouts of the walls and roof pieces, before working with the actual gingerbread. And be sure to adjust the quantity of gingerbread to conform to your plan.

The gingerbread house is best made over two days. The first day (starting early to allow the gingerbread time to cool and harden), make the gingerbread, cut it into the desired geometrical shapes, and construct the house using the royal icing. The second day, make the almond blocks and the nut sablés, and decorate, adding any other confections you want.

Day 1

GINGERBREAD

1½ cups honey	*1 tablespoon ground cinnamon*
1½ cups sugar	*1 tablespoon ground ginger*
6 tablespoons butter	*1½ tablespoons ground cardamom*
6 tablespoons lemon juice	*1½ teaspoons ground cloves*
3 tablespoons grated lemon zest	*6 tablespoons baking powder*
7½ cups all-purpose flour	*2 eggs*

Preheat the oven to 350°F. In a large saucepan, combine honey, sugar, and butter, and bring to a boil. Add the lemon juice and zest, and remove from the heat to cool. In a large mixing bowl, combine the flour, spices, and baking powder, and stir to blend. Stir about one-third of the flour mixture into the honey combination, add the eggs, and continue to stir until blended. Work in the remaining flour mixture as you stir. When all of the flour mixture is added, continue to work the batter until it is smooth. Press the batter into three 11- by 17-inch shallow sheet trays, and bake for 35 minutes or until dark brown.

As soon as the gingerbread comes out of the oven, cut it into the desired shapes with a knife or pastry wheel. While still soft, carefully remove the pieces to wax paper with one or two wide spatulas, and allow them to cool thoroughly. Meanwhile make the royal icing. *Makes 3 11- by 17-inch sheets of gingerbread.*

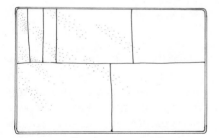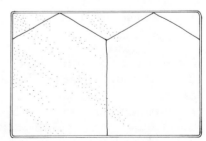

Two 11 x 17 inch trays - cut for Victorian Gingerbread House

ROYAL ICING

3 ½ cups confectioners' sugar
½ teaspoon cream of tartar
3 to 4 egg whites

Sift the sugar twice. Beat together the sugar, tartar, and egg whites to a smooth consistency. Keep icing covered with a damp cloth as you work.

Once the gingerbread is thoroughly cool and hard, you may begin construction. Fill a pastry bag, fitted with a #4 tip, with royal icing. Lightly score the base of gingerbread where you are going to position your walls. Take any one of the walls, squeeze the royal icing along the bottom edge, and position it. Hold it in place until it stands by itself. Squeeze royal icing on the bottom edge and adjoining side edge of either adjoining wall and attach. Continue until all walls are standing and firm. Smear the back of the thin strips of gingerbread and attach, where you feel appropriate, as bay windows. Squeeze the icing on only one edge of the roof where it will attach to the other side of the roof along the peak. Join both halves of the roof on top of the house, but do not attach the roof to the house. This will make it easier to attach the almond block shingles the next day. Let the construction harden overnight. Sprinkle a little water on your leftover royal icing, cover, and allow to sit overnight at room temperature. You may have to make more icing.

Day 2

ALMOND BLOCKS (Shingles)

½ cup sweet butter
¾ cup packed light brown sugar
2 large eggs
¼ teaspoon almond extract
1 cup bread flour
¾ cups cake flour
2 teaspoons unsweetened cocoa
½ teaspoon baking soda
2 cups sliced almonds

Preheat your oven to 350°F. In a large mixing bowl, cream together the butter and sugar until smooth. Add 1 egg, almond extract, both flours, cocoa, and baking soda, and mix until thoroughly blended. Add 1¼ cups almonds and stir in by hand. Turn the dough out and shape it into a 9- by 3- by 1-inch brick. Refrigerate it until firm. Cut the dough in half lengthwise. Line up the bars side by side and cut into ¼-inch thick slices. Place the dough slices on a paper- or parchment-lined cookie sheet. Beat the other egg with 1 tablespoon water, brush the tops of the dough slices with this wash, and decorate each with an almond slice. Bake for 8 minutes or until firm.

You may either stop here and put the shingles on your house; or you may stop here and eat all the shingles; or you can go on and make the nut sablés. To attach anything to the house you simply need a squirt of icing.

NUT SABLÉS (Window Panes, Door Panels)

½ cup sweet butter

½ cup confectioners' sugar

1 cup all-purpose or cake flour

1 large egg white

½ teaspoon vanilla extract

¼ teaspoon ground cloves

⅛ teaspoon ground cinnamon

⅛ teaspoon grated nutmeg

Pinch of salt

½ cup roasted hazelnuts, chopped fine

5 ounces semi-sweet chocolate

1 teaspoon vegetable oil

Preheat the oven to 350°F. Cream the butter and sugar until smooth. Add the flour, egg white, vanilla, spices, salt, and hazelnuts. Continue to mix until well blended.

Shape the dough into three rectangular bars of about 4½ by 1½ by 1 inch as best you can. Then slice each bar into ¼-inch thick slices. Put the dough slices on a cookie sheet lined with paper and bake for 20 minutes or until light brown.

Heat the chocolate and oil over simmering water until the chocolate melts. Dip each cookie diagonally, halfway into the melted chocolate, and set aside on parchment or brown paper until the chocolate hardens. *Yields 4½ dozen.*

Make more royal icing if you need it. Remove the roof from the house and set aside while you decorate the house. Using the icing, simply squirt a dab on the back of the almond block cookies and attach to the sides of the house to create a shingle effect. Then use the nut sablés to create windows and doors. Squeeze icing over the top edges of all four walls and attach the roof. Use the almond blocks to shingle the roof, also. If you like, create a snow effect on the roof and the base with extra icing. Attach candies at this point, if you have them. And use the remaining cookies however you like. You may even eat them—they're delicious.

Modern Europe and America

Ginger and the Decline of Spice Use in the West

While ginger was still on the ascent in Africa and Latin America, by the late seventeenth century the European craze for ginger began to subside. Colonial America's Dutch, German, and English settlers brought their passion for ginger to the New World, but this passion waned as in their homelands.

Ginger's decline in popularity was part of a general decline in the use of spices in European cooking. The flavor of the spices had always been secondary to their value as preservatives, medicinal tonics, and to some extent, luxury items for ostentatious display. Once fresh foods became more available, and there was relief from the plague and other diseases that had decimated the population, spices lost some of their magic. In fact, the prestige of being able to obtain foods with flavors that did not have to be masked replaced the prestige of being able to afford exotic Asian spices. The spices were also more available, and therefore less precious.

A fashionable rebellion of sorts was waged against spiced foods. In America, meat, which had often been consumed in a putrid state by medieval ancestors, was eaten barely cooked (rare). Certainly it was a matter of taste, but it was also a sign that one could afford a piece of meat that could be eaten unadulterated.

Changing social mores also affected the spicing of foods. In England, as the lusty Elizabethans gave way to the Puritans, and later the Victorians, the unabashed use of aphrodisiacs became frowned upon. Ginger's cousins, galangal and grains of paradise, disappeared from England and the rest of Europe altogether. Many aspects of life that were once "spicy" or "racy" were simply no longer accepted.

Ginger in Europe Today

In modern Europe, ginger is found in the foods, such as spice breads, confections, and preserves, that remain from earlier eras. Of the preserved meats, once ubiquitous, Europeans have retained their fondness for sausages, terrines, and pâtés. Ginger's use as a sweetmeat continued, and may even be on the upswing if Australia succeeds with its new confections.

India's influence on the food of England has brought new uses for ginger, turmeric, and cardamom to the West. Pickles, relishes, and spicy table condiments like Worcestershire sauce seem almost Western. Curry powders, which are mixtures of spices commonly used in India, are in fact a Western convenience. Indian cooks use the same spices, but never in prepackaged blends.

Holland has maintained a close though not always warm relationship with Indonesia since 1610; consequently ginger is as prominent in Dutch cooking as any in Europe. The Dutch even use it fresh, in a very popular rice dish known as *kerrieschotlge*. Besides dishes of obvious Indonesian influence, the Dutch make unusual uses of ginger, such as a cocktail snack that combines Gouda cheese, fresh pineapple, and candied ginger. Another appetizer is *bitterballen*, meatballs made with ginger.

Most curious is the lack of ginger in modern Italian cooking, considering the craze for it in the Roman Empire, Venice's control of the spice trade, and Italy's proximity on the Mediterranean to the Middle East. Wavery Root indicated at least an Italian awareness of ginger when he explained that in certain areas of Italy, when a dish is described as "strong," it means dominated by ginger. *Panforte* presumably is an example, but contemporary recipes do not call for ginger. (There is an Italian mineral water bottled with ginger, called "ginger soda." See page 158.)

The United States

In the early 1800s Salem, Massachusetts was the world's number one spice port, and this country consumed a lot of ginger. This was true, in fact, for 200 years after the first settlers arrived. Candied ginger, ginger cookies, ginger ice cream, and gingerbread were all eaten in abundance. It was as thoroughly an American spice as any, to the point of its inclusion in the rations provided to American soldiers during the Revolutionary War.

In modern America fresh ginger is rapidly becoming part of our cooking heritage. More than a nouvelle cuisine fascination, ginger is a staple for tens of thousands of Americans. Most of these are newly arrived from Asia and Latin America, and to satisfy their demand we grow some of the world's finest ginger in our fiftieth state, Hawaii. Fresh ginger is now available by the ton and becoming more available by the day. Because of our new fascination with fine fresh foods and our country's history of rapid Americanization of everything that reaches these shores, it will soon be difficult to remember when we did not cook with this strange-looking rhizome from Asia.

STEAMED PRAWN MOUSSE • East/West

There is a burgeoning movement—a fad at this point—to combine the foods of the East and the West. The following Western mousse, steamed in Eastern fashion, falls under this category. However, its combination of butter and cream with fresh ginger and coriander elevates it above a mere contrivance. Serve it with a vegetable and a salad.

2 pounds prawns (or shrimp), shelled and deveined

2 large eggs

½ cup heavy cream

1 teaspoon ginger juice

1 tablespoon cornstarch

1 tablespoon dry sherry

1½ teaspoons salt

½ teaspoon white pepper

Sauce:

2 teaspoons finely minced garlic

1 tablespoon minced fresh ginger

2 tablespoons minced shallots

2 tablespoons sweet butter

1 cup fresh peeled, seeded, and chopped tomatoes (or canned Italian plum tomatoes)

1 teaspoon salt (less if using canned chicken stock)

½ cup chicken stock

1 cup heavy cream

½ teaspoon white pepper

Sprigs of fresh coriander for garnish

Cut the shrimp into pieces and place in a blender or food processor with the rest of the mousse ingredients. (If a blender is used, reserve the eggs and cream and add them at the end just to blend.) Transfer the paste to a mold or flame-proof dish (approximately 3-cup capacity) that has been greased. Fill bottom of a wok or large pot with water and put in steaming rack. Bring water to a boil. Place mold or dish on rack and steam, covered, for 30 minutes.

Meanwhile, begin the sauce. Sauté the garlic, ginger, and shallots in the butter until the shallots are translucent. Add the tomatoes and salt and simmer for 5 minutes. Add the stock and cook over medium-high heat, stirring frequently, until the sauce is reduced by half. Stir in the cream and cook for about 10 minutes, until the sauce is lightly thickened and creamy. Sprinkle in the pepper, cover to keep warm, and turn off the heat.

To test whether the mousse is done, insert a skewer into its center. If done, the skewer will come out clean. Unmold the mousse onto a serving platter, pour the sauce over it, garnish with the coriander, and serve. *Serves 4-6.*

Fresh Ginger at Thanksgiving

If fresh ginger were used at Thanksgiving, the definitive "American" meal, it could revolutionize all of "American" cooking. At least that was my thinking when I conceived of putting together a Thanksgiving meal using ginger in every dish. But I reconsidered and stopped short of tampering with the turkey, fearing that to do this would be to commit a blasphemous act! I settled for the cranberry sauce and pumpkin pie. Fresh ginger gives a lift to pumpkin pie. Simply substitute one tablespoon of juice and 1 tablespoon of minced ginger per half teaspoon of ground ginger in your favorite recipe. Those who want to add another gingered dish to their feast might consider the Moroccan Sweet Potatoes with Saffron and Cinnamon on page 115.

CRANBERRY SAUCE WITH WALNUTS • *America*

1 pound fresh cranberries
1¾ cups sugar
⅓ cup finely shredded fresh ginger
Grated rind of one grapefruit ⟩ or orange
⅓ cup grapefruit juice
½ cup coarsely chopped walnuts

In a saucepan, combine all ingredients except the walnuts. Cover and bring to a boil. Reduce the heat and simmer until the cranberries split open, about 10 minutes. Set aside.

Toast the walnuts on a baking sheet in the oven for 10 minutes at 350°F. When cool, add them to the cranberry mixture. Chill before serving. *Makes about 3 cups.*

Two Pork Roasts

These two pork loin roasts are historically unrelated as far as I can tell, save for their dependence on ginger. One is Jamaican and uses rum and brown sugar; the other is a Swedish favorite, pork roast with prunes, *Plommonspäckad fläskkarré*.

PORK ROAST WITH RUM • *Jamaica*

1 center cut pork loin, 5 to 6 pounds, with bones

4 cloves garlic, cut into slivers

1 tablespoon fresh ginger in ½-inch slivers

20 cloves

2 teaspoons salt

1 teaspoon freshly ground black pepper

6 tablespoons dark rum

1 cup brown sugar

1 teaspoon ground ginger

2 cups chicken stock

Juice and grated peel of one large lime

1 tablespoon cornstarch mixed with ¼ cup water

Preheat the oven to 450°F. Score the fat side of the loin in a cross-hatch pattern of 1-inch diamonds, ½-inch deep. Poke holes all over the surface of the meat with the tip of a sharp knife. Insert 2 or 3 garlic and ginger slivers in each hole, and poke the cloves into the meat at evenly spaced intervals. Rub the salt and pepper all over the meat. Roast on a rack at 450°F for 30 minutes. Turn the heat to 325°F and roast for another 30 minutes.

Meanwhile, blend two tablespoons of the rum with the brown sugar and ground ginger.

After 1 hour, take the pork out of the oven, but leave the heat on. Pour the stock into the roasting pan to deglaze it, and leave the stock in the pan. Rub the pork with the brown sugar mixture and return it to the oven for 45 minutes. When the roast is done, remove it from the oven and let it rest while you prepare the sauce.

Pour the liquid from the bottom of the roasting pan into a saucepan. Warm the remaining rum in a small skillet. Take it off the heat and ignite it. Tilt the skillet back and forth until the flame goes out and add the rum to sauce. Add the lime juice and peel to the sauce. Bring the sauce to a boil, and add the cornstarch mixture after giving it a quick stir to recombine it. Stir and cook the sauce until it thickens, and correct the seasonings.

Slice the pork and arrange the slices on a platter. Serve the sauce on the side. *Serves 6-8.*

PORK ROAST WITH PRUNES · Sweden

2 dozen unsulfured dried prunes
1 center cut pork loin, 5 to 6 pounds
  (with bones)
1 tablespoon ground ginger

2 teaspoons salt
1 teaspoon freshly ground black pepper
½ cup water

Pit the prunes and put them in a mixing bowl. Cover with hot water and let them sit for 30 minutes.

Preheat the oven to 450°F. With a long, thin-bladed knife, make a pocket in the center of the loin. (You may have to work from both ends.) Make a 1-inch slit, but avoid cutting out the meat. Stuff the pocket (a sharpening steel works well for this) with the prunes. Combine the ginger, salt, and pepper and rub the pork with the mixture. Roast 30 minutes at 450°F. Turn the heat to 325°F and cook 1 hour and 15 minutes longer. Remove the roast from the oven and deglaze the pan with the water, stirring and scraping the bottom. Turn the meat and put it back in the oven for another 30 minutes.

Allow the roast to rest for 15 minutes before carving. Serve the meat sliced, with the pan gravy on the side. *Serves 6-8.*

CURRIED BROCCOLI SOUP WITH CREAM · America

This satisfying, lightly spiced cream soup works equally well with asparagus and a garnish of blanched asparagus tips. Serve warm, or chilled in the summer.

1 small bunch broccoli (about
  1 pound), trimmed and peeled
¼ cup sweet butter
1 large onion, sliced
1 tablespoon coarsely chopped ginger
1½ teaspoons curry powder, curry
  paste, or garam masala

1 quart chicken broth
1 cup cream
½ cup milk
1½ teaspoons salt, or to taste
½ teaspoon white pepper

Cut away about 12 flowerets of broccoli with skinny stems for garnish. Heat a cup of water to boiling in a small saucepan. Cook the flowerets for 2 minutes, then rinse under cold water and set aside. Cut the rest of the broccoli into 2-inch pieces and set aside.

Heat the butter in a large saucepan. Add the onion, ginger, and curry spices, cooking until the onions are wilted.

Add the broth and the broccoli pieces and bring to a boil. Cover, lower the heat, and simmer for 30 minutes. Puree this mixture in a food processor or blender, or run it through a food mill.

Reheat this mixture. Stir in the cream, milk, salt, and pepper. Turn off heat. Serve garnished with the reserved flowerets. If the soup is to be served cold, chill it thoroughly after mixing in the final ingredients. *Serves 4-6.*

PEAR CHUTNEY • *America*

Chutney (and pickle) recipes were brought to America by the English, who got their recipes directly from India, where chutney implies the use of ginger. Traditional American chutneys can be enlivened, practically restored, by substituting fresh ginger for powdered. The exchange rate should be one tablespoon of chopped fresh ginger, or more if you like, to half a teaspoon ground ginger.

5 cups diced pears (½-inch cubes)

½ cup coarsely chopped fresh ginger

4 cloves garlic, smashed

1 cup chopped onion

1 pound brown sugar

1½ cups cider vinegar

½ cup fresh lemon or lime juice

10 fresh red chili peppers, seeded and diced

3 limes, chopped whole

2 orange peels, cut into ½-inch cubes

1 grapefruit peel, cut into ½-inch cubes

½ pound raisins

2 cups diced pineapple, preferably fresh

2 cinnamon sticks (about 2 inches each)

2 teaspoons nutmeg

½ teaspoon ground cloves

2 teaspoons salt, or to taste

1 teaspoon white pepper

Put the pears, ginger, garlic, onion, sugar, vinegar, and lemon juice in a large saucepan to simmer for 5 minutes. Add the rest of the ingredients and simmer for 15 to 20 minutes. Store in jars in the refrigerator for up to six months. *Makes 2 quarts.*

GINGER ICE CREAM • East/West

Ginger ice cream was an early American favorite, although not much has been eaten for the past hundred years or so. It is making a comeback in new recipes that call for the Chinese preserved ginger in syrup or other types of candied ginger. Alice B. Toklas included an especially decadent version called Singapore Ice Cream in her cookbook, and there is a fine one in Barbara Tropp's *The Modern Art of Chinese Cooking*. The one below, with honey, was created for this book by ice cream enthusiast and friend Mimi Luebbermann, who suggests serving it with toasted almonds and chocolate sauce.

4 eggs
1 quart light cream
½ cup honey
¼ teaspoon salt
1 tablespoon vanilla extract
1 6-ounce jar preserved ginger in syrup
2 cups whipping cream

Combine the eggs, light cream, honey, salt, and vanilla and beat lightly. Put a cup of the mixture in a food processor or blender with the ginger and its syrup and process until the ginger is in small chunks. Add this to the egg and cream mixture; then add the whipping cream, and combine. Chill thoroughly (to get the greatest volume of ice cream), and freeze in an ice-cream freezer according to the manufacturer's directions. *Makes 2 quarts.*

BEVERAGES, CANDY, AND MEDICINE

Tea and Coffee;
Medieval Waters

Ginger Ale and Beer

Candied Ginger

Medicinal Properties

Remedies

Ginger Beverages

At one time or other ginger has added its piquancy and flavor to man's favorite liquids. Its history intertwines with those of tea, coffee, wine, beer, distilled spirits, liqueurs, and, of course, soft drinks. At first it was simply steeped, fresh or dried, in water, to be used as medicine; or it was juiced and blended with other medicinals for specific ailments. It became an early additive to fermented beverages. Beyond embellishing their tonic value, ginger, valued as a detoxifier, was thought to cut down the chances of being poisoned from these early brews. Ginger wines, with a base of fermented grains, were used in sacrificial rites in ancient China.* In India and the Middle East, ginger drinks with long medicinal histories are still popular. Talmudic scriptures and the Koran both mention refreshing gingered beverages.

Tea and Coffee

Tea and coffee have long been spiked with this rhizome. Ginger and tangerine peel were the first two flavorings added to Chinese tea during the T'ang Period (A.D. 618-907), when tea drinking became widespread. This preceded the more modern habit of perfuming teas with flower blossoms. The peoples of Ethiopia and Yemen were the first to drink coffee and the first to combine it with ginger. Sweetened, spiced coffee was being enjoyed throughout the Arab world for centuries before coffee was adopted by Europeans.

Honey Drinks

Many of the earliest fermented beverages—the medicinal honey wines, the *tej* of Ethiopia, the *hydromel* of ancient Greece, and the Anglo-Saxon *mead*, to name a few—were heavily laced with ginger and other spices. *Metheglin*, peculiar to Wales, traditionally called for boiling honey, water, and whole races of ginger.

Medieval Waters

While it takes some digging to find ginger liqueur these days, finding a liqueur or cordial without ginger in the Middle Ages was practically

---

* The most interesting was a turmeric wine of the early Chou Period (twelfth century B.C.–second century B.C.) that required court employees devoted exclusively to its manufacture and the rituals of its presentation.

impossible. Early liqueurs, known as composed waters, were medical potions, and cordials were by definition for the heart. Their fluctuating and often lengthy lists of ingredients combined distilled spirits and wine with ginger, galangal, and sometimes cardamom among other spices and herbs. Liqueurs specifically for the plague added zedoary, a turmeric. Grains of paradise, the African cardamom, seasoned most liqueurs, as a matter of course, for its ability to "rid the shaking fits, being drunk with Sacke (sherry)."[1] Benedictine is one of a handful of these medicinal waters to have survived intact since 1510.

Wine

The thought of adulterating a fine vintage Bordeaux would make many of us cringe. However, prior to the late eighteenth century (which takes in most of wine history), there were no such aged wines. What was drunk was highly acidic, and was spiced, sweetened, and usually consumed for health. Hippocrates was an early advocate of wine with spices, primarily ginger and cinnamon, and recipes for spiced wines, known as *hippocras*, lingered in English cookbooks until the 1830s, or about the time aged dry wines became popular. Mulled wines, and spiced wines such as Swedish *glogg*, often employing ginger, are the survivors of that tradition.

Ginger Beer and Ale

As might be imagined, there was ginger ale before Canada Dry or even Canada. Gingered beer probably can be traced to beer's origins in the Middle East. The first sloggy grain ferments needed a purifying spice, since they were without the benefit of reliable yeasts. The English, most decidedly, have long had an affinity for the combination of ginger and beer. One simply went with the other, thus enabling Elizabethan audiences to appreciate Shakespeare's fool during a raucous scene in *Twelfth Night* when, in referring to ale, he says "ginger shall be hot i' th' mouth." A supply of ground ginger was always available in British taverns for sprinkling in one's ale or porter—a habit that persisted until just before World War II.

The alcoholic drinks known interchangeably as ginger beer and ginger ale were first popularized by the British. They imported a taste for this type of beer to their colonies in the Caribbean where their slave cooks adapted recipes using fresh ginger in place of the bruised, dried rhizome, and lime instead of lemon. Rum was sometimes added after the initial stages of fermentation. Variations of these frothy, pungent brews spread along the slave routes throughout the West Indies and Latin America.[2]

Soft Drinks

The ginger ale we know today, a combination of ginger extract, carbonated water, sugar, and other flavorings,[3] is a faint echo of the sweet spiced soft drinks that became popular sometime after English chemist Joseph Priestly invented carbonated water at the end of the eighteenth century. In the 1880s, J. J. McLaughlin, a Toronto pharmacist, met with moderate success selling soda water to fountains and a dark ginger concentrate to go with it. The mixture approximated a well-known alcoholic ginger ale of Belfast, Ireland. In 1904, McLaughlin's fortunes increased considerably when he bottled a light and dry version and marketed it as "the Champagne of ginger ales." Its success was due to its acceptance as a mixer, or tonic. What Mr. McLaughlin had accomplished, in effect, was to bring medieval medicinal notions about spice and spirit mixtures into the twentieth century.

As ginger ale became synonymous with "light carbonated mixer" (the British poured it into real ale and called the result a shandygaff), heartier versions called ginger beer appeared.[4] Though not as successful, the latter is credited with helping to spread the popularity of vodka from Hollywood to the rest of the United States via the "Moscow mule," the invention of a California restaurateur with an excess of ginger beer.

Ginger Beverages Today

Besides today's array of soft ginger ales and beers, there are several English brandies, liqueurs, and wines featuring ginger. Among the most popular is a sweet currant wine bottled by Stone's. The Italians bottle a mineral water with ginger and orange bitters, known as "ginger soda," that is relatively pleasant.

NOTES—GINGER DRINKS

1. From sixteenth-century English herbalist John Gerard via Karen Hess in her notes for *Martha Washington's Booke of Cookery.*
2. The Indians of Nicaragua make a powerful *chicha*, a liquor from fresh ginger, as well as the more traditional corn *chicha* distilled by many Latin American Indians.
3. Since soft ginger ales were members of a broader category of tonic waters, they included several spices. Today's Canada Dry in fact uses, besides oleoresins and oils of ginger, vanilla, clove oil, cassia bark, rose oil, and citrus oils.
4. A September, 1983 *New York Times* article reports that ginger beer is making a comeback. The brand responsible, again out of Canada, is "Old Tyme," a nearly natural brew, slightly cloudy, with a bit of a bite, I suspect from capsicum.

MIGLEE • *Syria, Lebanon*

This healthful spiced drink is served to new Arab mothers to restore strength. Visitors who stop by to see the baby share *miglee* as a kind of toast to the mother's and child's health. Similar post-partum ginger beverages, broths, and stews are found in other cultures (see Pigs' Feet with Ginger and Black Vinegar, page 68).

2 whole dried ginger rhizomes
2 cinnamon sticks
2 whole cloves
1 tablespoon anise seeds

4 cups water
½ cup blanched almonds (preferably the small Asian variety, which are more flavorful)
½ cup sugar

Crack the rhizomes with a kitchen mallet or other heavy object, and add them to a pan with the cinnamon, cloves, anise seeds, and water. In a mortar or blender, blend the nuts and sugar together to form a paste, and add it to the pan. Bring the mixture to a boil, turn down the heat, and simmer for 30 minutes. Pour through a mesh strainer into a teapot or pan, pushing through as much of the solids as possible with the back of a spoon. Serve hot. *Serves 4-6.*

QISHR (Coffee with Ginger) • Yemen

In the South Yemen city of Mocha (a name with a familiar ring), coffee is a major export item, so valuable in fact that it is priced out of the range of most citizens. Instead, they consume gallons of *qishr*, a beverage made from the ground husks of coffee beans flavored with a healthy dose of ground ginger and sweetened with sugar. The following recipe is a variation of *qishr*, for those who cannot get husks.

1½ cups cold water
3 tablespoons dark-roast coffee

3 tablespoons sugar
1 tablespoon ground ginger

Put the water in a coffee pot that can stand a direct flame. Add the coffee, sugar, and ginger, and bring to a boil. Remove from the heat; when the bubbling stops, return it to the heat and bring to a boil again. Repeat this a third time, then let it rest for 2 minutes. Serve the *qishr* in demitasse cups or in the even smaller Arabic cups. *Makes 3-4 demitasse servings.*

COFFEE RAS-EL-HANOUT • Morocco

Ras-el-Hanout is a spice blend for which the amounts and varieties of ingredients vary (see Ginger in Morocco). The following version for coffee, from Paula Wolfert's comprehensive *Couscous and Other Good Food from Morocco*, is guaranteed to add an extra dimension to your favorite blend of coffee. Note that it incorporates not only ginger, but its cousin galangal.

2 whole nutmegs, or a heaping table-
*   spoon ground*
1 teaspoon ground cinnamon
6 dried rosebuds (optional)*
12 cloves, or ½ teaspoon ground
Pinch of gum arabic (optional)*
1 tablespoon ground ginger
½ teaspoon laos *powder*

Pinch of allspice
¾ teaspoon white pepper
½ teaspoon mace
15 cardamon pods
1 teaspoon fennel seeds
1 teaspoon anise seeds
1 tablespoon sesame seeds

Grind the spices and seeds that need to be ground in a blender or spice grinder. Put the entire mixture through a sieve into a jar that can be tightly sealed. Use ½ teaspoon of *ras-el-hanout*, or more to taste, for every ½ cup of coffee grounds and brew it however you like. *Makes about ½ cup.*

* Available in markets that sell Middle Eastern foods.

SPICED TEA (Masala Chah) · India

There are numerous combinations of herbs and spices that are added to the sweet spiced teas of India and the Middle East. A slice of fresh ginger alone in your favorite tea is a pleasant and digestively helpful way to end a meal.

4 cups cold water

1/3 cup milk or light cream, or to taste

4 quarter-sized slices fresh ginger

2 inches cinnamon stick

4 whole cardamom pods

3 cloves

3 tablespoons sugar, or to taste

2 sprigs spearmint (optional)

2 tablespoons leaf tea

Bring the water and milk to a boil and add the ginger, spices, sugar, and mint. Turn off the heat, cover the pan, and allow to steep for 15 minutes.

Add the tea, and again bring the mixture to a boil. Simmer for 5 minutes. Correct the sugar and light cream to your liking and strain into a warm teapot. *Serves 4.*

REAL GINGER BEER · Caribbean Islands

This brew is popular in a number of Caribbean Islands. Rum is an optional, though common, addition. English versions use dried ginger, lemon, and a bit of cream of tartar to aid the brewing process. Older English ginger and yeast brews used black treacle (molasses), and were known as treacle ales.

1/4 cup coarsely grated ginger, with the juice

Grated peel of two limes

6 tablespoons fresh lime juice

1 cup light brown sugar

4 cups boiling water

1 teaspoon active dry yeast

1/4 cup lukewarm water (about 110°F)

1/4 cup light rum, or more to taste (optional)

In a large ceramic bowl, combine the ginger, lime peel, lime juice, and sugar, and pour in the boiling water.

In a small bowl, sprinkle the yeast over the lukewarm water and let stand 2 minutes; then stir the yeast until completely dissolved. Set the bowl in a warm place until it begins to bubble, about 5 minutes. If it doesn't bubble, start over with fresh yeast.

Add the yeast mixture to the large ceramic bowl, cover tightly with plastic wrap or aluminum foil, and let stand for one week in a warm, draft-free spot. Stir briefly every other day. If using rum, mix in after five days. At the end of the week strain the mixture into a quart glass or ceramic container and cork it.* Allow to stand for three days at room temperature, then chill before serving. In the islands it is served over ice. *Makes about 1 quart.*

WASSAIL BOWL • *England*

This traditional English Christmas punch, with its spices, ale, and sherry (sack), has its roots in medieval medicinal brews. The name "wassail" comes from a toast to good health. My editor, Jay Harlow, who is first and foremost a fine chef, came up with this version, after some research, to serve at a gingerbread tasting we held. We served it for tradition's sake (just before Christmas), as well as to test the recipe. To everyone's delight, it proved warming and delicious, and produced an unusual camaraderie. Wassail may become a tradition over the holidays in Berkeley, California.

12 tart cooking apples	*3 cloves*
¼ cup brown sugar	*3 allspice*
4 bottles stout	*1 cinnamon stick, crumbled*
4 bottles pale ale or lager	*2 teaspoons ground ginger*
1 fifth medium sherry	*Zest of 2 lemons*
½ teaspoon grated nutmeg	*12 eggs*
½ teaspoon cardamom seeds	*½ cup sugar*

Preheat the oven to 300°F. Core the apples, leaving the bottoms intact. Put a teaspoon of brown sugar in each cavity, place the apples in a buttered baking dish, and bake until soft, about 30 minutes. (This may be done ahead and the apples kept warm.)

Combine the ales and sherry in a large kettle and add the spices and lemon zest. Bring almost to a boil, stirring occasionally to release the foam from the ale, and simmer 5 minutes. Meanwhile, separate the eggs. Place the yolks in a large punch bowl and beat them lightly. In a separate bowl, beat the egg whites to the soft-peak stage, add the sugar, and continue beating until the whites are stiff but not dry. Fold the whites into the yolks in the punch bowl. Strain the hot ale mixture into the bowl, beating constantly. Add the baked apples. Serve the ale in punch cups. The apples can also be eaten. *Serves 24.*

---

* Follow precautions you normally would in bottling beer.

KRUPNIKAS • *Czechoslovakia*

This ginger- and turmeric-based liqueur turned up at the last minute. It was given to me by Charlotte Shimura, who got it from a woman from Utah who bottles it every year for Christmas gifts. How a Slavic liqueur of obvious medieval origins came to be made in Utah has yet to be explained. Besides the mystery of its journey, it is fascinating in that it shares a similar spice configuration with Eastern European spice breads.

2 rhizomes dried ginger
2 rhizomes dried turmeric
1 tablespoon caraway seeds
10 whole cloves
10 whole allspice
3 sticks cinnamon
1 vanilla bean
10 cardamom pods

½ whole nutmeg
Rind from one fresh orange
Rind from one fresh lemon
Pinch of saffron
4 cups water
2 pounds honey
1 quart 190-proof alcohol (sometimes called "everclear")

Crack rhizomes of ginger and turmeric with a kitchen mallet or other heavy object. Add with the rest of the spices to the 4 cups of water and bring to a boil in a saucepan. Turn the heat to low and simmer, uncovered, for about an hour. It should be reduced by half. Turn off the heat and allow to steep while you prepare the honey.

In another large heavy saucepan bring the honey slowly to a boil while skimming off the foam. Strain the spice water into the honey and remove from the heat. Slowly stir in the alcohol. Bottle and allow to age six months. *Makes 4 bottles (⅘ quart).*

Candied Ginger

F ew, if any, candied foods have a longer history than candied ginger. Marco Polo wrote of vendors hawking threads of sweetened ginger on Chinese streets. Many centuries before, the Chinese had launched this successful processed food by combining ginger with the first sweetener, honey. "Stem ginger in syrup" in the familiar green glazed crock, is the modern descendent, and the process has not been changed, save for the substitution of sugar syrup for honey.

Ginger as a sweetmeat was wildly popular in medieval and Tudor England where recipes specified the use of "green," meaning fresh, ginger. Taking a slice or two after meals was an early English habit which spread to colonial America, and continued until the craze for ginger subsided in the eighteenth century. More than satisfying the world's largest collective sweet tooth, it aided in the formidable task of digesting dinner in the Middle Ages.

Terminology

To alleviate some of the confusion regarding the terms for sweetened ginger, which are often used interchangeably, and to mitigate the surprise of those who grab just any old box of "preserved ginger" from the shelf of a Chinese grocery, I've provided the following:

Ginger in Syrup. The stems are the immature knobs of young ginger. These have been packaged in glazed pottery of varying quality down through the ages in China; antique "ginger jars" are often collectors' items. The familiar 14-ounce green crock of ancient design comes from the Tung Chun Soy & Canning Company of Hong Kong. Fancier versions are available in Oriental gift shops. The knobs are delicious simply chopped a bit and poured with their syrup over vanilla ice cream.

Crystallized Ginger. These are the familiar ginger slices which have been cooked in sugar syrup and coated with granulated syrup. Crystallized ginger is best made from ginger free of fiber, though to many tastes very young ginger does not provide enough flavor or bite.

Candied Ginger. Technically all sweetened gingers are candied, but in the West this refers to sweetened bits (*glacé*) without a sugar crust.

Preserved Ginger (Chinese). All ginger cooked in a sugar mixture is preserved, but when the Chinese label it "preserved ginger," it is not only sweetened but spiced with a good dose of salt and licorice rhizome, a common Chinese method of preserving plums and other fruit. Ginger preserved in this manner includes a variety of ginger confections oddly labeled in English, such as "Lemon Juice Ginger."

Sweetened Stem Ginger. Simply stem ginger or young ginger knobs processed in syrup and sold in plastic packages without the liquid. This specialty of Xinhui, China is sold under the Pearl River Bridge label.

Ginger Fudge. A spicy and addicting caramel-like candy from Indonesia that, in spite of its name, contains no chocolate. The individual red, white, and blue wrappings are of striking design.

HONEYED GINGER • *Ancient China*

Don Harper of the Department of Oriental Languages, University of California, Berkeley, who is researching ancient Chinese medicinal texts, contributed this, the earliest recorded method for candying ginger. The recipe is translated from a sixth century A.D. manual entitled *Essential Arts for the Equalization of the People.* I have included it more for illustrative than practical purposes, although it can be followed with success. (It is interesting to note that the early Chinese specified cuts, lengths, and quantities of ingredients, whereas in the West, recipes did not give quantities until relatively modern times.)

Wash clean one *chin* (224 grams or a little over ½ pound) of fresh ginger. Peel away the skin. Cut it into sticks the thickness of lacquer chopsticks, without worrying about the length. Place these in two *sheng* (1½ cups) of water and bring to a boil. Remove the scum. Add two *sheng* of honey, let it come to a boil again, and remove the scum. Remove the ginger sticks to a bowl (leaving the syrup in the pot, which is to be cooked so it reduces by half.) Pour the syrup over the ginger sticks and allow them to macerate. [These sticks are] to be used with chopsticks, for two people together. When there is no fresh ginger, use dried ginger. The method is as before, only it should be cut up very finely.

CRYSTALLIZED GINGER

Making your own crystallized ginger is easy, and it makes a nice gift. The combination of granulated sugar and the golden lumps of Chinese yellow rock sugar results in an unusually full-flavored, soft-textured candy with a golden hue. Using all granulated sugar, however, is perfectly acceptable.

1½ pounds very fresh ginger (avoid
    overly mature, fibrous rhizomes)
1⅓ cups granulated sugar
¼ pound Chinese yellow rock sugar
Salt
Water

Cover the ginger in cold water and soak overnight. Drain and cover again with fresh water and bring to a boil. Lower the heat and simmer for 10 minutes. Drain and allow to cool.

Peel the ginger and cut it into ⅛-inch slices; or if you choose, cut into sticks the width of thin, lacquered chopsticks, as did the ancient Chinese. Cover these pieces with water and simmer for 10 minutes. Drain and repeat this process; then drain again.

Put the sugars and a pinch of salt into a pan with 2½ cups of water. Bring this to a boil and simmer until the sugar is dissolved. Add the ginger pieces, bring to a boil again, and simmer for 5 minutes. Turn off the heat and allow to sit for at least an hour.

Finally, turn on the heat and simmer, stirring from time to time, for at least 30 minutes, or until most of the liquid is absorbed. Stir constantly at this point. When the ginger is nearly dry, remove the pan from the heat and continue to stir for another 5 minutes. Pluck out the pieces with chopsticks or small tongs and allow to cool and harden on wax paper.* Crystallized ginger will keep indefinitely in a sealed container. *Makes 1½ pounds.*

* Some of the ginger pieces may end up a bit damp or sticky, which is why crystallized ginger is typically coated with sugar. Feel free to toss these pieces in granulated sugar as they begin to cool, but use a light hand.

CHOCOLATE-COATED GINGER

In Europe, the availability of the mild, fiberless crystallized ginger of Australia has sparked a recent upsurge in the consumption of candied ginger. This resurgence parallels the new mania for chocolate; thus chocolate-coated candied ginger, by no means a new concept, is prominently displayed in specialty shops. In the United States, it can be found under the Bendicks label.

The recipe below was given to me by Anne Kupper of Williams-Sonoma, who brought a batch she had made to a recipe testing session. It works best with Australian crystallized stem ginger, which comes packaged in cubes, and a rich sweetened chocolate such as Callebaut of Belgium, available in bricks.

½ *pound rich, sweetened chocolate*
1 *pound crystallized stem ginger*
Toothpicks

Melt the chocolate in the top of a double boiler. Allow to cool so that it will generously coat the ginger. Insert a toothpick into a cube of ginger and swirl it in the chocolate until coated. Insert the other end of the toothpick into anything that will keep the confection from touching a surface while it cools and hardens (anything from a piece of foam board to a cucumber will serve as a stand). Repeat with the remaining ginger cubes. *Makes about 1½ pounds.*

Ginger as Medicine

Most cooks would not cite ginger's ability to alleviate nausea and curb flatulence as reasons for adding it to their Christmas cookies. But these are among a lengthy list of curative powers that made it widely popular.

"The plant which repels dampness" was the first definition for the character symbolizing ginger in Chinese.[1] Dampness was a major concern in ancient China. It was assigned responsibility for chills, ague, spasms, tetanus, and leprosy, among other ailments. Ginger was a major preventative, as well as a cure, for the illnesses caused by dampness and its metaphoric partner "wind," which were characterized by a loss of heat. The Chinese were certain that ginger's warming properties restored health.[2] This model of health as a balance of heat and cold spread throughout early cultures, as did the star tonics, such as ginger, that could maintain the balance or correct any imbalance. Our concept of a cold and the notion that we catch it from the elements stem directly from these first ideas of medicine.

Besides repelling dampness and wind, early texts cite ginger's cleansing and purifying properties. "When consumed for a long time [fresh ginger] eliminates body odors and puts a person in contact with the spiritual effulgences," according to the most ancient Chinese pharmacopaeia.[3] Beyond mere healing, the ability of ginger to cleanse and thus purify the system took on a spiritual dimension. Its consumption was permitted, even encouraged, by Confucius during the fastings from which more worldly seasonings were prohibited. Religious sects in India who shunned the use of onions and garlic (lest they offend the gods) not only consumed ginger, but used it in sacrificial rites. The idea that ginger leaves one internally clean and sweet-smelling, thus presentable to the gods, was not without empirical support. As the most refreshing smelling of seasonings, it was used by the Chinese and Indians to counteract any hints of rankness or foul order in food. It had been observed to calm the gastric rumblings linked to flatulence. It was known to induce perspiration, a cleansing and toxin-removing process, and to speed up blood circulation to the

167

same effect. And according to old herbal tracts, the skin of ginger contains a diuretic agent.

Centuries of empirical study have both refined and expanded the powers attributed to ginger, and have proven its medical validity to the satisfaction of many cultures. The founders of Western medicine, among them Dioscordes, who wrote *De Materia Medica* in A.D. 78, ascribed numerous medicinal abilities to ginger. It is still a top-ranking botanical in the Chinese pharmacopaeia, and is highly regarded in modern Japan where, in spite of the influence of Western medicine, over two billion dollars is spent annually on herbal remedies.

Medicinal Properties

There is no want of medicinal lore about ginger, though not a lot of what we call "scientific" testing has been done, at least in the West. Choosing which of its medicinal qualites to specify here has been a matter of finding a consensus. Roughly, if all the ginger-using countries of Asia, the Greeks and Romans, the Europeans of the Middle Ages, the Elizabethans, and other assorted converts, have agreed that ginger is good for a particular something, it is mentioned. This may be a letdown for those harassed by nocturnal sexual demons,* since it is an historical minority that swears a rhizome on the bedpost keeps them away.

Alleviates Nausea (antiemetic). Ginger prevailed over dramamine in a 1982 test of effectiveness in reducing motion sickness. But this is nothing new. England's Eliza Acton, in her 1845 *Modern Cookery for Private Families*, provides a recipe for a ginger loaf that is "excellent for 'disturbances of the stomach,' especially in travelling."[4] Sometime before the fifth century, Chinese sailors began bringing fresh ginger on voyages—which not only helped with seasickness, but also prevented the scurvy that debilitated Western sailors until they began using citrus to the same effect in 1600. It has long been the habit of Chinese chefs to chew ginger while working to prevent the nausea caused by the combination of long exposure to cooking odors and intense heat. (It also keeps their taste buds sharp.) Ginger has been recommended for centuries for the early morning nausea that accompanies the first stage of pregnancy—most recently, as I was writing this, by a doctor on a radio talk show here in San Francisco.

Aids Digestion (stomachic, carminative). Ginger's ability to calm stomachs has been held in high regard for centuries. Candied ginger was the routine sweetmeat served at the end of the meal in England and Colonial America, a habit with some precedent. Ginger was the

* *Succubi and Incubi.* A problem which either doesn't exist or has been effectively closeted in modern America.

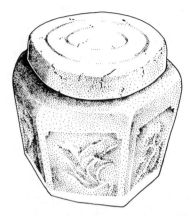

Alka-Seltzer of the Roman Empire, which, evidently, needed all the help it could get. It was prominent in their "aromatic salts," whose function according to Apicius was "for the digestion, and to move the bowels." The people of India who rely on hard-to-digest legumes rely on fresh ginger. The early Chinese reasoned that a kind of toxin which ginger attacked was responsible for upset stomachs, and deduced that ginger's curative powers extend to food poisoning. In modern Chinese guides to medicinal herbs, ginger is still considered an antidote and preventative, especially for shellfish poisoning, one of the reasons ginger is always served with crab.

Prevents Colds, Aids Symptoms (expectorant). Most cultures prescribe warming liquids to combat colds and chills; in Asia they add ginger. Its constant use is felt to be a preventative, and if a cold or the "flu" is contracted, ginger alleviates symptoms, particularly in the accumulation of phlegm in bronchial conditions, and speeds recovery. Its perspiration-inducing warmth is valued in "sweating out" a fever. Raw peeled ginger dipped in warm water and rubbed on the backs of children is a modern as well as ancient treatment for bronchial congestion akin to the warming "rubs" of the West.

Restores Appetite (sialogogue). Beyond curbing nausea, ginger stimulates the flow of saliva, and is recommended to be taken in some form before meals for loss of appetite.

Helps with Menstruation Difficulties; Quickens Post-Partum Recovery. Ginger is thought to be particularly effective in maintaining women's health. Ginger has long been recommended for irregular menstruation. Various post-partum soups, stews, drinks, and mixtures featuring ginger are common from the Far East to the Near East. These are shared ritually with the visitors who drop by. The Cantonese share a pigs' feet and ginger stew (see page 68); Syrians down a spiced beverage called *miglee* (see page 158).

Stimulates Lustful Yearnings (aphrodisiac). This quality, which may well have sold more ginger than all other qualities combined, has been the hardest to prove. It does stimulate circulation, and has, for a fact, spiced up the language (see page 26). Regardless of its effectiveness, it has been characterized as an aphrodisiac from ancient Asian tracts to Arabia's *The Thousand and One Nights*, the writings of the Greek physician Dioscordes, and the famous 1597 *Herball* of Englishman John Gerard, whose description of ginger as "provoking Venerie" comes as a warning. There is probably no connection, but the countries which have used the most ginger, China and India, have the largest populations.

Works Externally (rubefacient). Ginger also stimulates blood flow when applied externally. It is a common massage medium in China and Japan, its warming properties serving as a liniment for aching muscles. It is a common ingredient in compresses and poultices, where it is applied for everything from headaches to localized cancers. It will enhance a warm bath, or the penetrating properties of hot water for soaking sprained joints.

Remedies

Here is a sampling of simple, commonly used ginger cures. Unless otherwise specified, they are gathered from authoritative Asian herbal texts. Most of these texts are from governmental health agencies in China, which have been conducting a rigorous scientific examination of herbal medicines since the late 1950s. The only guarantee that I can make for the recipes is that they are not harmful, and that the results are not as tasty as the other recipes in this book.

None of these cures is designed to treat serious or persistent conditions, for which a doctor should be consulted. Nor are they strict in the sense that you cannot try your own variations, e.g., the addition of ginger slices or juice to the warming liquids that one might take for a cold. Ginger plays an important role in a number of standard herbal formulas available in Chinese drug stores, none of which are included here.

A Manhattan neurosurgeon I knew swore by a ginger-laden formula he bought over-the-counter in Chinatown for hangovers, a condition I hoped was not chronic to him. To the same effect, divide a teaspoon of ginger juice between two glasses of your morning orange juice and drink them both.

Fresh Ginger Slices. For a nauseous stomach, mild food poisoning, or to help perspiration flow when sweating out a fever. Simmer three

¼-inch slices of fresh ginger in 2 cups of water for 30 minutes. Drink one cup of the hot liquid three to four times a day until the condition is improved.

Variation # 1. To stop a cold or flu in the early stages, add 1 tablespoon of brown sugar to the above dose.

Variation # 2. For a severely nauseated stomach and vomiting, before simmering the ginger slices stir-fry them in a wok or skillet until they are lightly browned.

Fresh Ginger Juice. To break up phlegm and stop coughing, grate enough fresh ginger to produce ½ teaspoon of juice. Strain juice into a cup of water. Dissolve and drink three to four times a day.

Dried Ginger. For a stomach cold, or what we sometimes call 24-hour flu (the symptoms of which include vomiting, diarrhea, chills, and lowered blood pressure), or a chest cold with congestion and coughing, simmer ½ ounce of dried ginger slices (available in Chinese herbal shops; or do it yourself, see page 37) in 2 cups of water for 30 minutes. Drink a cup at a time, three times a day.

Burned or Fried Ginger. For diarrhea or for irregular menstrual bleeding, stir-fry ¼ ounce of dried ginger slices in a dry wok or skillet until they blacken on the outside and are light brown inside; then simmer them in 2 cups of water for 30 minutes. Drink a cup at a time, three times a day.

Powdered Ginger. For suppressed or retarded menstruation, dissolve ½ ounce of powdered ginger in a pint of boiling water. Allow to cool, and take ½ teaspoonful every two hours.

Ginger and Parched Rice. For indigestion, soak ½ cup plain white rice overnight, drain, then cook in a dry wok or skillet until golden brown. Boil 1 teaspoon of the rice with a ¼-inch slice of fresh ginger in a cup of water. Turn off the heat and allow to steep for 5 minutes. Strain and drink. (Save the rest of the rice for other occasions.)

EXTERNAL APPLICATIONS

Ginger Juice. To massage tired, aching muscles or sore joints: grate ½ pound of fresh ginger into a cheesecloth, strain the juice, dip fingers in the juice and rub it into affected areas.

As a variation, mix fresh ginger juice with an equal quantity of sesame oil and use as above.

Roasted Fresh Ginger. For headaches, heat a piece of fresh ginger over a flame or in the oven until hot. Remove and cut off several thin slices. Apply the warm slices to the affected area. Change slices when they cool.

Ginger Compress. For localized aches, pains, bruises, and cysts, squeeze ½ cup of grated ginger through cheesecloth into 3 quarts of water kept just below boiling. Dip a small towel into the water, wring it out, and apply it to the area to be treated. As the towel cools, repeat for a total of 15 minutes. The ginger water may be used once more within 24 hours.

Ginger Bath. For tired aching feet, arthritic or bursitic pain, or aching muscles or joints, soak the affected parts of the body (or take a full bath) in hot water using the juice from ½ cup of grated ginger (squeezed through cheesecloth) for every gallon of water.

NOTES—GINGER AS MEDICINE

1. Information found by Don Harper, of the Department of Oriental Languages, U.C. Berkeley, in a first century A.D. etymological dictionary, *Shou Wen Chieh Tzu (Explication of Graphs and Analysis of Words)*.
2. For further information see "Ginger is Heat," in Ginger in China, page 51.
3. *Shen Nung Pen Ts'ao (Materia Medica of the Divine Agrarian;* ca. 2nd century A.D.).
4. Professors Dennis Clayson, of Ohio, and Daniel Mowray, of Brigham Young University, who studied thirty-six people susceptible to motion sickeness, by giving them either ginger, dramamine, or a placebo, as reported by the *San Francisco Chronicle*.

APPENDIX

*To Grow Your Own
Ginger*

To Grow Your Own Ginger

A feature article in the Sunday Leisure section of *The New York Times* (January 1, 1984) pointed out that with a little fussing to make it sprout, a ginger houseplant is easy to maintain. The sprouting process takes up to six weeks or longer, and, given the availability of fresh ginger, it would seem that growing your own to eat is silly. But for those who want a new and unusual house plant, Bonnie Fisher, the culinary herb authority who wrote the piece, recommends:

1. Carefully select a firm piece of fresh ginger with plenty of knobs.

2. Use either a top-grade commercial soil mixture, or combine equal parts sand, vermiculite, compost, and rich garden loam. Plant the rhizome horizontally in a large clay pot with ample room both around and below for the new tubers to grow. Cover the ginger with only one-half inch of soil.

3. Put the pot over a steady source of heat, such as a radiator or water heater; water the rhizome thoroughly and continually for several weeks to get it to sprout. Once it sprouts, move it into the light and reduce the amount of watering. The soil may be nearly dry between waterings. It may be fertilized once a month with a mild fertilizer. In the summer, the plant may be put in a sunny, wind-protected spot on your porch.

BIBLIOGRAPHY

Aero, Rita. *Things Chinese.* Garden City, N.Y.: Garden Books, 1980.

American Spice Trade Association. "What You Should Know About Ginger." New York, 1980.

Apicius. *The Art of Cooking,* translated as *The Roman Cookery Book* by Barbara Flower and Elizabeth Rosenbaum. London: Peter Nevill Ltd., 1958.

"A Sparkling Story" and "The Story of Canada Dry," publications of the Canada Dry Company.

Brennan, Jennifer. *The Complete Thai Cookbook.* New York: Richard Marek Publishers, 1981.

Burros, Marian. "The Short Life of Fad Foods." *The New York Times,* December 10, 1983.

Buderim Ginger Growers Co-op Association, Ltd. "Merrybud Golden Ginger." Queensland, Australia: School Project Bulletin.

Chang, K.C., ed. *Food in Chinese Culture.* New Haven: Yale University Press, 1977.

Chinese Massage Therapy. New York: Cloudburst Press, 1983.

Claiborne, Craig, and Virginia Lee. *The Chinese Cookbook.* Philadelphia and New York: J.B. Lippincott, 1972.

David, Elizabeth. *English Bread and Yeast Cookery.* London: Penguin, 1978.

David, Elizabeth. *Spices, Salts and Aromatics in the English Kitchen.* New York: Penguin, 1981.

Davidson, Alan. *Fish and Fish Dishes of Laos.* Rutland, Vermont, and Tokyo: Charles E. Tuttle Co., Inc., 1975.

Devi, Gayatri. *Gourmet's Gateway—The Maharani of Jaipur.* India: private publication.

Dupaigne, Bernard. *Le Pain.* Paris: Editions de La Courtile, 1979.

Eason, Yla. "Ginger Beer and Amiance." *The New York Times,* September 4, 1983.

Fisher, Bonnie, "Ginger Roots Yield Double Dividends: A Beautiful Plant Plus Fresh Flavor." *The New York Times,* January 1, 1984.

Gansu New Pharmacological Institute. *Herb Pharmacology.* Beijing: People's Health Publishing House.

"The Ginger Cure." *San Francisco Chronicle,* December 12, 1982.

"The Ginger Story: Cultivation, Processing, Marketing. Report of India's Spice Enquiry Committee, India: January, 1955.

Grigson, Jane. The Art of Making Sausages, Patés, and Other Chacuterie. New York: Alfred A. Knopf, 1976.

Grossman, Harold J. Grossman's Guide to Wine and Spirits, update by Harriet Sanbeck. New York: Charles Scribner and Sons, 1983.

Guenther, Dr. Ernest. "Ginger Production in Jamaica." The Flavor Field Section, Coffee and Tea Industries, Part I, December, 1958; Part II, January, 1959.

Hazelton, Nika Standen. The Cooking of Germany. New York: Time-Life Books, 1969.

Hess, Karen. Martha Washington's Booke of Cookery. New York: Columbia University Press, 1981.

Hsu, Dr. Hong-yen and Douglas H. Easer. A Practical Introduction to Major Chinese Herbal Formulas. Los Angeles: Oriental Healing Arts Institute, 1980.

Jaffrey, Madhur. An Invitation to Indian Cooking. New York: Alfred A. Knopf, 1973.

Keys, John D. Chinese Herbs. Rutland, Vermont, and Tokyo: Charles E. Tuttle Co., 1981.

Kuo, Irene. The Key to Chinese Cooking. New York: Alfred A. Knopf, 1977.

Kushi, Michio. Cancer and Heart Disease: The Macrobiotic Approach to Degenerative Disorders. Tokyo: Japan Publications, 1982; dist. Harper and Row.

Leonard, Jonathan Norton. Latin American Cooking. New York: Time-Life Books, 1968.

Li, Hui-Lin. "The Vegetables of Ancient China." Economic Botany: 1969.

Lichine, Alexis. Alexis Lichine's Encyclopedia of Wine and Spirits. New York: Alfred A. Knopf, 1968.

Lin, Hsian Ju, and Tsuifeng Lin. Chinese Gastronomy. New York: Pyramid Publications, 1972.

Lü Shih Ch'un Ch'iu (Spring and Autumn of Master Lu). Third century B.C.

Mallos, Tess. The Complete Middle East Cookbook. New York: McGraw Hill, 1983.

McKay, Ronald. "Gingerly Does It." Baker's Revioew. Australia: September, 1982.

Montagne, Prosper. "Quatre-Épices." Larousse Gastronomique. New York: Crown Publishers, 1961.

Ok, Cho Joong. *Home Style Korean Cooking in Pictures*. Tokyo: Japan Publications, 1981.

Ortiz, Elisabeth Lambert. *The Complete Book of Caribbean Cooking*. New York: M. Evans and Company, Inc., 1973.

"Pain d'Épice." *Strasbourg Museum Catalog*.

Pinsuvana, Malulee. *Cooking Thai Food in American Kitchens*. Bangkok: Sahamitr Industrial Printing, 1976.

Root, Waverly. *Food*. New York: Simon and Schuster, 1980.

Sahni, Julie. *Classic Indian Cooking*. New York: William Morrow and Company, Inc., 1980.

Seeley, Charles. *Ginger Up Your Cookery*. London: The Anchor Press Ltd., 1977.

Shih-Chen, Li. *Chinese Medicinal Herbs*, translated by F. Porter Smith and G.A. Stuart. San Francisco: Georgetown Press, 1973.

Sing, Phia. *Traditional Recipes of Laos*. London: Prospect Books, 1981.

Singh, Dharami. *Indian Cookery*. London: Penguin Books, 1971.

Smires, Lafita Bennani. *Morrocan Cooking*. Paris; Editions Jean Pierre Tallandier, 1972.

Sonakul, Sibpan. *Everyday Siamese Dishes*. Bangkok: Chatra Press, 1952.

Steinberg, Rafael. *The Cooking of Japan*. New York: Time-Life Books, 1969.

Stobart, Tom. *Herbs, Spices and Flavorings*. Woodstock, N.Y.: The Overlook Press, 1982.

Sunset's New Western Garden Book. Menlo Park: Lane Publishing Company, 1979.

Tannahill, Reay. *Food In History*. New York: Stein and Day, 1973.

"Traditional German Christmas Cookies." *Food and Wine*. December, 1979.

Tropp, Barbara. *The Modern Art of Chinese Cooking*. New York: William Morrow and Company, Inc., 1982.

Tsuji, Shizuo. *Japanese Cooking, A Simple Art*. Tokyo: Kodansha International, 1980.

van der Post, Laurens. *African Cooking*. New York: Time-Life Books, 1970.

Wolfert, Paula. *Couscous and Other Good Food from Morocco*. New York: Harper and Row, 1973.

Yule, Henry and Burnell, A.C. *Hobson-Jobson: A Glossary of Colloquial Anglo-Indian Words*. 1903.

INDEX

Caraway seeds, in liqueur, 162
Cardamom (*Amomum; Elettaria* spp.), discussed, 24, 75
  African. *See* "Grains of Paradise"
  black (*Alpinia allughas; Amomum amarum; Zingiber nigrum*), 37n.3
    (*Elettaria cardamomum* var. *major*), 24
    in India, 93
    in Moroccan cooking, 108
  green. *See* Cardamom pods, green
  pods: in coffee, 159
    in liqueur, 162
    in tea, 160
    green: with braised chicken, 98; in India, 93; in Morocco, 108
  as medicine, in Japan, 84
  seeds, in Wassail Bowl, 161
  in *speculaas*, 139
Caribbean, ginger beer in, 156-57, 160
Carrot: relish, fresh, 105
  in tempura pancakes, 87
  with zucchini, 72
Casserole, a Chinese, 66
Cashew nuts, in *vatapa*, 127
Cayenne. *See* Pepper, cayenne
Celery (Chinese; "Napa") cabbage, discussed, 44
  with meatballs, 66
  and white turnip salad, 71
Central America, ginger in, 123
Chan Heng (Chinese poet), 51
Chats (cold appetizers), 95
Chenel, Laurie, 65
Chermoula (Moroccan marinade), 109
  for fish, 111
Chicha (fresh ginger liquor), 158n.2
Chicken: in apricot and coriander sauce, 98
  giblets: stir-fried, 80
    in tajine, 112
  legs, Moroccan grilled, 114
  with mint, basil, and peanuts, 80
  with olives and preserved lemons, 113
  in peanut stew, 125-26
  preparation of, in India, 95
  with prunes, honey, and almonds, 112
  skinning, discussed, 99n.
  soup, spicy, 82-83
  tajine, 108
  white-cooked, with ginger and scallion sauce, 64
Childbirth, restoratives after, 54, 68, 158, 169
Chili oil. *See* Oil
Chili pepper (chilis), discussed, 41
  with braised duck, 128
  in chicken soup, 82
  in chutney, 152
  dried, discussed, 44, 48

  in celery salad, 71
  with lamb, 97
  in potato soup, 104
  in pickle, 73
  fresh, discussed, 94
    with eggplant, 101
    in peanut stew, 126
  green: in carrot relish, 105
    in potato soup, 104
    in *vatapa*, 127
  with green beans, 102
  with grilled fish, 111
  to handle, 41
  in peanut stew, 126
  in picadillo, 130
  red: in cucumber pickle, 73
    with squid, 62, 124
    in tajine, 112
Chili paste with garlic, discussed, 44
  in steamed fish, 60
  in stir-fried chicken, 80
Chilis. *See* Chili pepper
China: galangal in, 23
  ginger in, 51-56
    cultivation of, 29
    dried, 31
  influence of, on Southeast Asian cooking, 76
  medicine in, 121
    ginger in, 118-19, 170
    government research on herbal, 170
  recipes from, 58-74
  tea, with ginger, 155
  turmeric in, 22
  use of ginger in ancient, 24, 155, 164, 167
Chinese Cookbook, The (Lee), 70
Chinese rock sugar. *See* Sugar, Chinese
Chocolate: -covered ginger, 166
  for nut sablés, 145
Chopsticks, 53
Chutney: fresh, 105
  in Indian cooking, 96
  pear, 152
Cinnamon, discussed, 46
  sauce (*cameline*), 122
Claiborne, Craig, 70
Classic Indian Cooking (Sahni), 99n.
Clementine peel, candied, 138
Cloves, discussed, 46
Coconut: cream, for fruit salad, 132
  fresh, discussed, 41, 94
  milk: canned, 45, 79
    discussed, 45
    to make fresh, 45
    unsweetened, 104, 127
Coffee: bean husks, 159
  dark roast, 159
  with ginger, 155, 159

Fagara. *See* Sichuan peppercorns
Fannie Farmer Baking Book (Cunningham), 140
Fats, ginger and, 55
Fennel seed, 46
  in coffee, 159
  in eggplant pickle, 106
  in steamed fish, 60
Filo pastry, Moroccan, 110
Fiji, ginger from, 28
Fish: to broil, 111
  ginger with, 54, 85
  grilled with marinade (*chermoula*), 111
  lime-mint deep-fried, 77-78
  in Moroccan cooking, 109
  steamed whole: Cantonese, 58
    Shanghai-style, 59
    Sichuan home-style, 60
  types of, for steaming, 57-58, 60
  in *vatapa*, 127-28
  whole fried, 77
Fish sauce, fermented, (*nam pla; nuoc mam; tuk trey*), discussed, 46
  with fried fish, 77
  with ginger flowers, 81
  with stir-fried chicken, 80
Fisher, Bonnie, 174
Five-flavors (Chinese), and ginger, 55
Five-spice powder, discussed, 46, 56
  with duck, 65
Flounder, for steaming whole, 57, 59
Flour: pastry, for *speculaas*, 139
  rye, 137- 138
Flowers, ginger, 75, 81
Food poisoning, ginger as a preventative of, 169
France, recipe from, 138
Fruit, tropical, in salad, 132

Galen, 118
Galingale. *See* Galangal
Galangal (*Alpinia* and *Kaempferia* spp.) (galingale), discussed, 23-24, 37n.3, 75
  in charcuterie, 121
  dried. *See Laos* powder
  in Europe, 146
  fresh, 23, 76
    in chicken soup, 82
    using, 79n.
  in Japan, 84
  lesser (*Kaempferia pandurata*) (Camphor root; Indian ginger; *kentjur; krachai*), 23-24, 37n.3, 76
  as medicine, 84
  in Morocco, 108, 109-10
  wild, in India, 93
Garam masala, discussed, 46
  for green beans, 102
  for lamb curry, 97

to make, 46
for potato salad, 100
in soup, 151
Gari (sushōga) (pickled ginger), 84, 85-86, 90
Garlic, discussed, 41
  ginger and, 55, 86
Garnishes. *See also* Condiments
  for chicken soup, 82
  for Chinese noodles, 69
Gerard, John, 26, 37n.6, 170
Germany, gingerbread in, 135, 136
Ginger (*Zingiber officinale*), 21, 29, 75, 84, 107n.2
  in Africa, 123
  ale, 157
  "baby" (young), 27-28
    with squid, 62
  bath, 172
  beef (real), 70
  beer, 156-58
  beverages, 155-62
  blushing, 24
  burned, medicinal, 171
  candied, 121, 163-66
  candy, with pinenuts, 91
  in Central America, 123
  in Chinese cooking, 52-55
  chocolate-coated, 166
  compress, 172
  confectionary, 32. *See also* Ginger, candied
  crystallized, 164-66
  for curing meat and fish, 53
  decline in popularity of, 146
  dried: in braised chicken, 98
    in Chinese food, 56
    to grind, 30
    ground, 30-31, 94, 98, 171
    "hands" of, 30
    in liqueur, 162
    to make, 37
    medicinal use of, 30-31, 84, 171
    in Middle Eastern cooking, 107
    in *miglee*, 158
    in Morocco, 108-10
    as a substitute for fresh, 115
  in East Africa, 120
  in Egypt (ancient), 107
  in Ethiopia, 120
  etymological origin of, 120n.
  in Europe, 121, 147
  extract, 32
  fresh: to buy, 27-29, 33-34
    to crystallize, 165
    to dry, 37
    freezing, 34
    in Korea, 86
    in modern American cooking, 148
    to prepare, 35-36

Vinegar: black (sweetened), discussed, 44
  with crab, 61
  with pig's feet, 68
  substitute for, 61
 Chinese. *See* Vinegar, black
 cider: in chutney, 152
  in pickled eggplant, 106
 rice: discussed, 47
  for *sushōga*, 90
 sweetened. *See* Vinegar, black
Vodka, and ginger beer, 158

Walnuts, in cranberry sauce, 149
Warka (Moroccan filo pastry), 149
Wasabi (green horseradish), 36, 84n.
  grater for, 85
Washington, Mary Ball (George's mother), 141
Wassail Bowl, 161
Water chestnuts, discussed, 49
  fresh, 49
  as medicine, 52
West Africa. *See also* Slaves, cooking of
  peanut stew in, 125
  recipes from, 124, 125-27
West Indies: ginger beer in, 157
  recipe from, 131
Western cooking, ginger and, 118-23
Wine: ginger in, 156

honey, with ginger, 155
 mulled, with ginger, 156
 turmeric, 155n.
Wine rice. *See* Rice, fermented, sweet
Wok, 42, 76
Wolfert, Paula, 23, 47, 110, 113

Yeast, active dry, in ginger beer, 160
Yemen, the: coffee with ginger in, 155
  recipe from, 159
Yin-yang: ginger and, 53-54, 61
  in Japanese food, 84
Yogurt: in potato soup, 104
  in *raitas*, 96, 105
Yugoslavia, gingerbread in, 136

Za jiang mein (noodles with bean sauce), 53, 69
Zanzibar, recipe from, 128
Zedoary (*Curcuma zedoaria*), 22
  in India, 93
  in liqueurs, 156
Zingiber officinale. See Ginger
  Z. mioga. See Ginger, mioga
  Z. nigrum. See Cardamom, black
Zingiberaceae leaves of, 75
Zinj, the plant of, 120
Zinjabil, 120
Zucchini, with carrot, 72

Notes

Notes

Cookbooks from Aris Books/Harris Publishing Company

The Book of Garlic by Lloyd J. Harris. The book that started America's love affair with garlic. It consolidates recipes, lore, history, medicinal concoctions and much more. "Admirably researched and well written."—Craig Claiborne in *The New York Times*. Third, revised edition: 286 pages, paper $9.95

The International Squid Cookbook by Isaac Cronin. A charming collection of recipes, curiosities and culinary information. "A culinary myopia for squid lovers."— *New York Magazine*. 96 pages, paper $6.95

Mythology and Meatballs: A Greeek Island Diary/Cookbook by Daniel Spoerri. A marvelous, magical travel/gastronomic diary with fascinating recipes, anecdotes, mythologies and much more. "A work to be savored in the reading."—*Newsweek*. 238 pages, cloth $16.95, paper $9.95

The California Seafood Cookbook by Isaac Cronin, Jay Harlow and Paul Johnson. The definitive recipe and reference guide to fish and shellfish of the Pacific. It includes 150 recipes, magnificent fish illustrations, important information and more. "One of the best manuals I have ever read."— M.F.K. Fisher. 288 pages, cloth $20.00, paper $11.95

The Feast of the Olive: Cooking with Olives and Olive Oil by Maggie Blyth Klein. A complete recipe and reference guide to using fine olive oils and a variety of cured olives. 223 pages, cloth $16.95, paper $9.95

The Art of Filo Cookbook by Marti Sousanis. International Entrees, appetizers and desserts wrapped in flaky pastry. 144 pages, paper $8.95

Chevre! The Goat Cheese Cookbook by Laurel Chenel and Linda Siegfried. A marvelous collection of international recipes using goat cheese. 119 pages, paper $8.95

To receive the above titles, send a check or money order made out to Aris Books for the amount of the book plus $1.25 postage and handling for the first title, and 75¢ for each additional title. To receive our current catalogue of new titles, send your name and address plus 50¢ for postage and handling.

ARIS BOOKS 1621 5th Street, Berkleley, CA 94710 (415) 620-0254